CHINESE MUSIC HANDBOOK

How to write Chinese Style Music

Brian Voon Yee Yap

First Published in 2021
by Brian Voon Yee Yap
Monbulk, Victoria, Australia
© 2021 Brian Voon Yee Yap

978-1-922465-69-6 (paperback)
978-1-922465-70-2 (ebook)

My thanks and appreciation to those who assisted with the production of this book: Kirsten Leah, Barry Crockett, David Munroe, Amanda Collins, and Catlin Bush

INTRODUCTION

This book is written as a guide for people who know the western staff notation and want to know about writing music that sounds like traditional Chinese music.

This book is split into two parts. The first part describes the techniques needed to create Chinese style music. The second part is about the underling theory of the notation systems and pitch selection.

The Chinese music system is quite prescriptive. Of course, you do not need to follow it. But if you do, you will be on the path to have music that sounds like traditional Chinese music.

I have used simplified Chinese characters in the main book. The table of terms gives the complex Chinese character equivalents.

WHAT IS CHINESE MUSIC?

What you think of as to being Chinese music is very personal. Chinese music could be a folk song; it could be the music for a court ritual; it could be an elaborate operatic piece; it could be a group participating in a lion dance.

Chinese music has a history of over six thousand years of development. In that time, it has changed over and over again. But some underpinnings have remained remarkably constant.

Written Chinese music tends to only record the basics of the tune. The musician is expected to know how to perform a piece and how to embellish it. This interpretation varies from player to player; it varies from region to region; it varies between the purposed of the music; it varies from instrument to instrument, and it varies over time.

You should treat this book as a "good place to start". I have endeavored to cover off on what might be considered Chinese common practice.

The most understood part of Chinese Music, in the west, is the Pentatonic Scale. The Pentatonic Scale is a foundation stone of the music. Often western composers will include some pentatonic parts to give the impression of Chinese music.

This example, taken from the Turandot Overture written by Carl Maria von Weber in 1809, shows the parts of Chinese Music that are well understood in the west. The pentatonic sale is used, the piano uses staccato to imitate a zither and parallel octaves are used.

There is much more to Chinese Music. Apart from the different sounds emanating from the different instruments: There are different ways that the melodies are structured and assembled; There are different ways to compose rhythm; and, in particular, there is the use of percussion which is very different to the use of percussion in any Western Music.

This book is split up to describe Chinese Music as follows:

1. Chinese Scales (page 3)
2. Pentatonic Intervals (page 13)
3. Pentatonic modes (page 14)
4. Harmony (Page 52)
5. Switching keys (Page 53)
6. Beat and Time (Page 54)
7. Beat Groupings (Page 55)
8. Rhythmic groups (Page 67)
9. Percussion (Page 67)
10. Drum Notation (Page 71)
11. Melodies and Chords (Page 73)
12. Melodies (Qǔpái, 曲牌) and Suites (Page 96)
13. Inverse scale modes (Page 100)
14. Notation Systems (Page 100)
15. Tuning (Page 102)
16. Glossary of Terms (Page 105)

CHINESE SCALES (SHĒNGYĪN JIĒ - 聲音階)

Chinese Music focuses primarily on the five-note pentatonic scale. Other scales are hexatonic (six note) and heptatonic (seven note).

The basic terminology is:

12 Tones	are the twelve tones of a twelve-tone system. Over thousands of years, a variety of ways of determining these pitches have been developed and I have included more on the tuning systems at the end of this book.
5 Notes	are the five notes of the pentatonic scale. This is sometimes translated as five steps.
7 Notes	are the seven notes of the heptatonic scale. This is sometimes translated as seven steps.

PENTATONIC SCALES (WǓ YĪNJIĒ, 五音階)

The main pentatonic scale used in standard music in China have varied over time. The pentatonic scale documented here is the major pentatonic scale. This is the scale most used in the current era. In earlier times, the lydian mode pentatonic scale was the predominant scale used. I have also seen rare mentions of aeolian pentatonic scales being used.

TONAL PENTATONIC SCALE (QUÁNYĪN WǓ SHĒNGYĪN JIĒ, 全音五聲音階)

In modern Chinese Music the major Ionian Mode Pentatonic Scale is the scale most commonly used. The notes, starting with the tonic, are called gōng (宮), shāng (商), jiǎo (角), zhǐ (徵), and yǔ (羽). In the C Major Key, the notes are: C, D, E, G, and A.

These Five-Tone Scale notes are called the Positive Notes (Zhèngyīn Jí, 正音级).

OTHER PENTATONIC SCALES

In older Chinese Music the Lydian Pentatonic Scale was the most commonly used scale. In the C Major Key, it consists of the notes: F, G, A, C, and D.[1]

---

[1] This is effectively the same as the F (Zhōng Lǚ, 仲呂) Major Key, if you avoid using the B flat that exists in the F major key.

The mixolydian mode is sometimes used. In the C Major Key, it consists of the notes G, A, B, D, and E.

Locrian is another rarer scale. The 7 is tuned a little flat and the 4 a little sharp[2]. Om the C Major Scale it consists of the notes B, C, D, F sharp, G and B flat.

The Semitone Pentatonic Scale (Bànyīn Wǔ Shēngyīn Jiē, 半音五聲音階) omits the third and fifth notes and keeps the fourth and seventh notes. This scale is different in that the standard pentatonic scales use steps of 2 and 3 semitones while this scale uses steps of 1, 2, and 4 semitones. In the C Major scale, it consists of the notes C, D, F, A, and B.

The Neutral Pentatonic Scale (Zhōnglì Wǔ Shēngyīn Jiē, 中立五聲音階) uses a sharp tonic and a flat tonic in the position of the fifth note of the Five-Tone Scale[3]. The tonic is shown as a half flat and the seventh is shown as a half sharp. This is because of the staff notation software used. The texts are quite vague as to the actual tuning of these notes. They just say, "a little sharp" or "a little flat". In the C Major scale, it consists of the notes C sharp, E, G, A and C flat.

In an early archaeological find the notes (in the form of tuned stone blocks) were split up into groups. The first group (shown in with a note head that is hollow with a cross) is the major five tone scale as would be played on white keys – that is in C Major (Huáng Zhōng, 黄钟) Key. The second group (shown in black) is the major Five Tone Scale as would be played on black keys – that is in F# Major (Ruí Bīn, 蕤賓) Key. The two notes left over shows as diamonds are the two changing notes. These notes allow you to change between the keys. They are shown in black.

---

[2] A little is ambiguous. If the tuning is a quarter tone, then we would get an Arabic scale.

[3] The Neutral Pentatonic looks like an Arabic Scale.

The remaining Scale Modes are listed here. They are not commonly used in Chinese Music. But they complete the set of pentatonic scales based on the modes of the heptatonic scale.

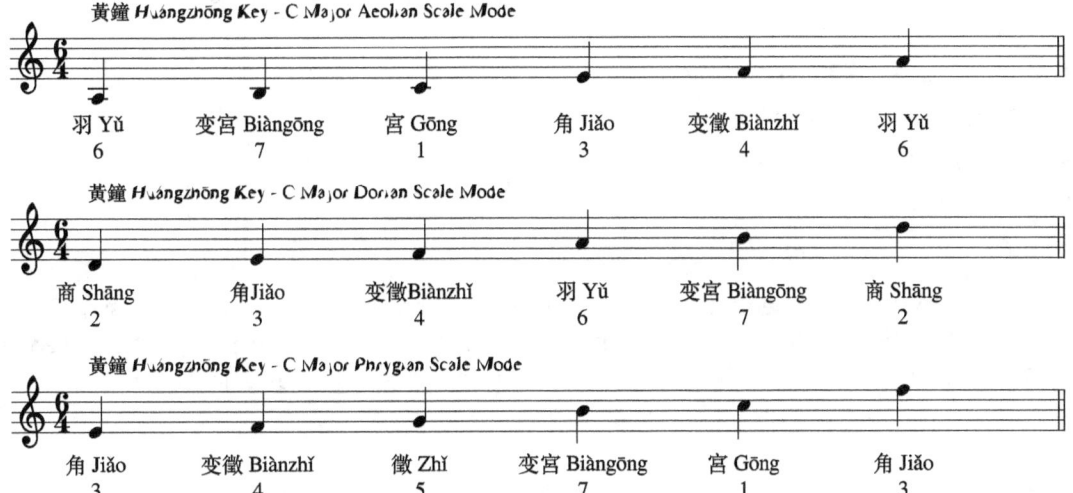

黃鐘 Huángzhōng Key - C Major Aeolian Scale Mode

羽 Yǔ	变宫 Biàngōng	宫 Gōng	角 Jiǎo	变徵 Biànzhǐ	羽 Yǔ
6	7	1	3	4	6

黃鐘 Huángzhōng Key - C Major Dorian Scale Mode

商 Shāng	角 Jiǎo	变徵 Biànzhǐ	羽 Yǔ	变宫 Biàngōng	商 Shāng
2	3	4	6	7	2

黃鐘 Huángzhōng Key - C Major Phrygian Scale Mode

角 Jiǎo	变徵 Biànzhǐ	徵 Zhǐ	变宫 Biàngōng	宫 Gōng	角 Jiǎo
3	4	5	7	1	3

In tabular form the step intervals are as follows.

Scale Mode	Steps
Ionian	M2-M2-m3-M2-m3
Dorian	M2-m2-M3-M2-m3
Phrygian	m2-M2-M3-m2-M3
Lydian	M2-M2-m3-M2-m3
Mixolydian	M2-M2-m3-M2-m3
Aeolian	M2-m2-M3-m2-M3
(Run)	M2-M2-m3-M2-m3
Locrian	m2-M2-M3-M2-M3

TABLE 1 STEPS FOR EACH SCALE MODE

For the scale mode steps – m2 is a minor second which is one semitone, M2 is a major second which is two semitones, m3 is a minor third which is three semitones, and M3 is a major third which is four semitones.

HEPTATONIC AND HEXATONIC SCALES

The following scales are or have been used in various regions and at various times.

- Biàngōng Yuè (变宫乐) is hexatonic;
- Qīng Jiǎo Yuè (清角乐) is hexatonic;
- Qīng Yuè (清乐) is heptatonic;
- Yǎ Yuè (雅乐) is heptatonic; and
- Yàn Yuè (燕乐) is heptatonic.

Even when the hexatonic and heptatonic scales are used, the primary tones are the five Positive Pentatonic Notes called Zhèngyīn Jí (正音级). The other notes are the one or two Changing Notes called Piān Yīn Jí (偏音级). In the music, these Changing Notes are used as passing notes or leading notes.

HEXATONIC SCALES (ZHÈNGYĪN JÍ, 正音级)

The Hexatonic Scales are called Zhèngyīn Jí (正音级). They are made up of the five Positive Tones (For C major: C, D, E, G and A) and one Changing Tone. The Changing Tone is used as passing note or leading note.

The Seventh Note Hexatonic Scale is called Biàngōng Yuè (变宫乐). It is made up of the five Positive Tones. The Changing Note is the seventh note.

The Sharp Third Note[4] Hexatonic Scale is called Qīngjiǎo Yuè (清角乐). It is made up of the five Positive Tones. The Changing Note is the fourth note.

---

[4] As a standard I use the flat fifth note form of the fourth note, but there is an enharmonic equivalent that is the sharp third note.

HEPTATONIC SCALES (TÓNG JŪN SĀN GŌNG, 同均三宫)

The three Heptatonic Scales are called Tóngjūn Sāngōng (同均三宫). They are made up of the five Positive Tones[5] and two Changing Tones. The three scales are differentiated by a combination of two of the following Changing Note options: (1) the fourth note or; (2) the sharp fourth note or; (3) the seventh note or; (4) the flat seventh note.

The scale names have been in flux for more than a century. The names I have included here are the current names, as best I can determine. Chinese academics are still arguing over the names.

This Major Heptatonic Scale is called the Lower Scale (Xià Zhēng Yīnjiē, 下徵音阶). The Changing Tones are the fourth and seventh notes. This scale is the same as a Western Major Scale, in the Ionian Scale Mode.

The Lydian Heptatonic Scale is called the Normal Scale (Zhèng Shēngyīn Jiē 正声音阶). The Changing Notes are the sharp fourth note and the seventh note. This scale is the same as a Western Major Scale, in the Lydian Scale Mode.

The Mixolydian Heptatonic Scale is called the Banquet Scale (Yàn Yuè, 燕乐音阶). The Changing Notes are the fourth note and the flat seventh note. This scale is the same as the Western Major Scale, in the Mixolydian Scale Mode.

---

[5] For C Major these are: C, D, E, G, and A.

CHINESE NOTE NAMES

There are two ways of naming notes. The key of the tune has one set of names and is determined using a system called the Twelve Pipes[6] (Shí'èr lǜ 十二律). Once a key is selected, the notes actually used in the tune are named as per the Five-Tone system.

MUSIC KEY (SHÍ'ÈR LǙ, 十二律)

The Twelve-Pipes system is only used to set the key of the tune. Changing the pitch of the key is called Rotating the Tonic (Xuán Gōng 旋宫).

Note	十二律		SHÍÈRLǙ	Interval	Chromatic Scale
1	黄	黄钟	Huáng Zhōng	Unity	C
#1	大	大呂	Dà Lǚ	Minor Second	C#/Db
2	太	太簇	Tài Cù	Major Second	D
#2	夾	夹钟	Jiá Zhōng	Minor Third	D#/Eb
3	姑	姑洗	Gū Xiǎn	Major Third	E
4	仲	仲呂	Zhòng Lǚ	Perfect Fourth	F
#4	蕤	蕤賓	Ruí Bīn	Tritone	F#/Gb
5	林	林钟	Lín Zhōng	Perfect Fifth	G
#5	夷	夷则	Yí Zé	Minor Sixth	G#/Ab
6	南	南呂	Nán Lǚ	Major Sixth	A
#6	无	无射	Wú Yì	Minor Seventh	A#/Bb
7	应	应钟	Yìng Zhōng	Major Seventh	B
+1	黄	黄钟	True Octave	Octave	C

TABLE 2 TWELVE PIPE TUNING TONIC NOTES

The staff lines below show the starting note of the key for each key in the first bar. The second bar shows the five pentatonic notes for that key. I have included the Number Notation (Jiǎnpǔ, 简谱) to emphasise that the 1 note, or tonic, changes for each key.

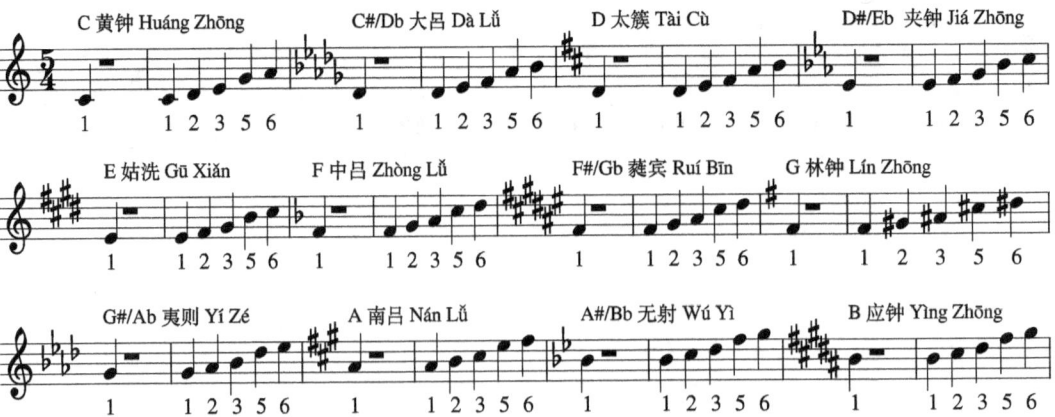

---

[6] It is called twelve pipes because in the past a standard set of Twelve Pitchpipes were used to set the pitch. These pitch pipes are the Chinese equivalent of a western tuning fork.

Examples: The first note of the Five-Tone System is note 1, Gōng (宫). In the music staff above this is represented by the number 1 in the Numbered Notation (Jiǎnpǔ 简谱).

1. For a tune to be played in the key of C: The Chinese Notation key is Huáng Zhōng (黄钟) and the tonic note for Gōng (宫) mode is C.
2. For a tune is to be played in the key of F: The Chinese Notation key is Zhòng Lǚ (仲吕) and the tonic note for Gōng (宫) mode is F.
3. For a tune to be played in the key of A: The Chinese Notation key is Nán Lǚ (南吕) and the tonic note for Gōng (宫) mode is A.

FIVE TONE NOTE NAMES (ZHÈNGYĪN JÍ, 正音级)

The five pentatonic Positive Notes (Zhèngyīn Jí, 正音级), starting with the tonic are called Gōng (宫), Shāng (商), Jiǎo (角), Zhǐ (徵) and Yǔ (羽). In the moving Solfège System[7], these same notes would be called Do, Re, Mi, So and La.

Sometimes there are the two changing notes. They are the fourth note (Biànzhǐ, 变徵) and the seventh note (Biàngōng, 变宫). With these two notes we have a full heptatonic scale. Biàn (变) means changed. So, the fourth note, Biànzhǐ (变徵) is a changed fifth note (Zhǐ, 徵); and the seventh note (Biàngōng, 变宫) is a changed first note (Gōng, 宫).

Jiǎnpǔ Note		Mode	Solfège
1	宫	Gōng	Do
2	商	Shāng	Re
3	角	Jiǎo	Mi
4	变徵	*Biànzhǐ*	Fa
5	徵	Zhǐ	So
6	羽	Yǔ	La
7	变宫	*Biàngōng*	Te
+1	宫	Gōng	Do

TABLE 3 FIVE TONE NOTE NAMES

---

[7] Solfège has two implementations: 1) A fixed implementation where Do is always C; and 2) A moving implementation where Do is the tonic note of the selected key. In this book the moving system is always used as it matches nicely to the Chinese mode system.

MODE SYSTEM (TÓNG GŌNG XÌTǑNG, 同宫系统)

The term *mode* has different definitions in Chinese Music and Western Music. Hence, I have adopted the following convention.

- Mode (diào, 调) is used to specify a Chinese Pentatonic Mode.
- Scale Mode is used to specify the Western Heptatonic Mode such as Ionian or Phrygian.

The process of changing to different modes is called Rotating the Mode (Zhuǎndiào, 轉調). Within the Mode System (Tóng Gōng Xìtǒng, 同宫系统) each Positive Tone can be the tonic. As a result, there are five modes. These five modes are called Gōngdiào (宫调), Shāngdiào (商调), Jiǎodiào (角调), Zhǐdiào (徵调), and Yǔdiào (羽调).

Note	Mode		Solfège	Semitone Steps				
1	宫调	Gōngdiào	Do	2	2	3	2	3
2	商调	Shāngdiào	Re	2	3	2	3	2
3	角调	Jiǎodiào	Me	3	2	3	2	2
5	徵调	Zhǐdiào	Fa	2	3	2	2	3
6	羽调	Yǔdiào	La	3	2	2	3	2

TABLE 4 CHINESE MODES

In this comparison table, I have included the Western Lydian and Locrian modes to complete the table. Lydian and Locrian have no Chinese mode equivalent.

Note	Mode		Interval	Scale Mode	Solfège
1	宫调	Gōngdiào	Unison	Ionian	Do
2	商调	Shāngdiào	Major Second	Dorian	Re
3	角调	Jiǎodiào	Major Third	Phrygian	Mi
4				*Lydian*	Fa
5	徵调	Zhǐdiào	Perfect Fifth	Mixolydian	So
6	羽调	Yǔdiào	Major Sixth	Aeolian	La
7				*Locrian*	*Te*
+1	宫调	Gōngdiào		Ionian	Do

TABLE 5 MODE COMPARISON

There are 84 modes in Chinese music. This is calculated from having the 12 starting notes and 7 modes per starting note. There is also a final note which can be any of the 7 notes in the scale. Not all 84 modes are used. Some sources suggest that about 60 of the modes are used.

CHORDS

The chords are built up from normal 12 TET (Twelve Tone Equal Temperament) triads for each pentatonic note. Only notes which are positive notes are allowed. If the note is not allowed, then the note is skipped, and the next allowed note is selected. I have included the letter "P" to indicate that the chord only has the pentatonic notes. For example, iiP is the second minor chord formed with only the pentatonic notes played. In this example the normal D minor chord is played as a D Minor Seventh with no third.

Two chords are shown in the following sections. The first chord is the 12 TET chord. The second is a pentatonic three note chord that omits the fourth and seventh notes because the notes are not part of the pentatonic chord.

A four-note pentatonic chord and a five-note pentatonic chord are shown in the musical notation.

C KEY CHORDS (HUÁNG ZHŌNG, 黄钟) - C TONIC – GŌNG MODE (宫调)

	Root	12 TET Chord		Pentatonic Chord	
宫	Gōng	C	I	C	IP
商	Shāng	Dm	ii	Dm7no3	iiP
角	Jiǎo	Em	iii	Em7no5	iiiP
徵	Zhǐ	G	V	Gsus2	VP
羽	Yǔ	Am	vi	Am	vimP

TABLE 6 BASIC CHORDS

Chords are shown as three note, four note, and five note chords.

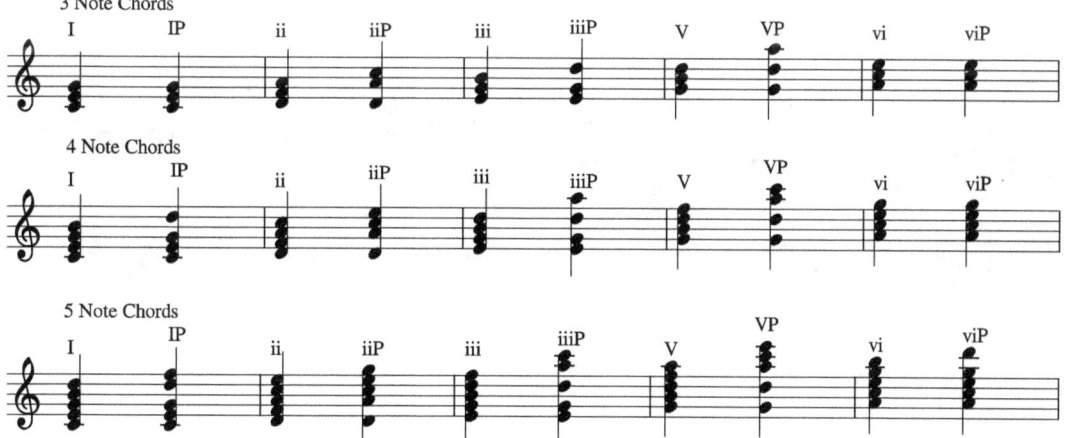

QUARTAL CHORDS

With a Five Note Scale we can create quartal chords of the positive notes by stepping down a fourth from the root note.

If we go up a fourth from the tonic note we get the two changing notes to complete a chord of the seven tones. Officially, you should only use a passing note in a chord if the chord is itself a passing chord.

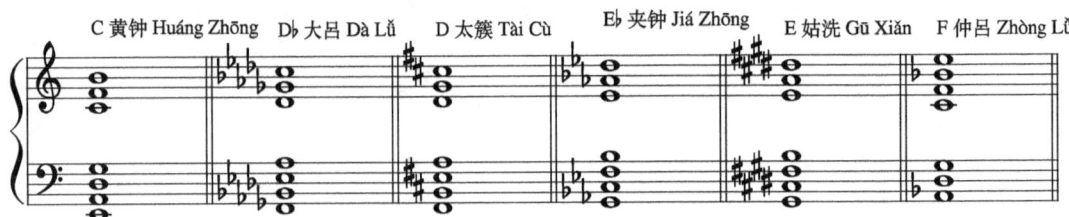

PENTATONIC INTERVALS

The intervals are based on the pentatonic notes only. Hence when measured in semitones the number of semitones is different to the ones that would be present in the Western Hexatonic scales. In these examples the root pitch is in the C Key (Huáng Zhōng, 黄钟) and the mode is Gōng Mode (宫调).

INTERVALS – SECONDS

In a Major Heptatonic Scale, the second intervals are either a Minor Second or Major Second creating a 2:1 ratio for the intervals. However, in the Major Pentatonic Scale the second intervals are either a Major Second or a Minor Third creating a 3:2 ratio for the intervals.

INTERVALS – THIRDS

In a Major Heptatonic Key, the third intervals are either a Minor Third or Major Third. However, in the Major Pentatonic Scale the third intervals are either a Minor Third or a Perfect Fourth.

INTERVALS - FIFTHS

In a Major Heptatonic Key, the fifth intervals are Perfect Fifths. However, in the Major Pentatonic Scale the third intervals are either a Perfect Fifth or a Minor Sixth.

INTERVALS – SIXTHS

In a Major Heptatonic Key, the sixth intervals are either a Minor Sixths or Major Sixths. However, in the Major Pentatonic Scale the sixth intervals are either a Major Sixth or a Minor Seventh.

PENTATONIC MODES (GŌNGDIÀO, 宫调)

Chinese Music modes are similar to Western Music modes.

Chinese Mode		Western Mode	
宫	Gōng	I	Ionian
商	Shāng	II	Dorian
角	Jiǎo	III	Phrygian
徵	Zhǐ	V	Mixolydian
羽	Yǔ	VI	Aeolian

For each stating note the following items are listed:

1. The modes,
2. The intervals,
3. The Chords,
4. The Chromatic Circle, and
5. The Key Scales.

There are enharmonic notes used in this section. The Chinese Music scale works up using sharps and no flats. The Western Music tradition the staff notation uses flat notes by convention for some scales. As we progress up the 12-Tone key notes the section titles stay true to the Chinese Music naming, but the examples given on the staff notation use the Western Music enharmonic equivalent.

Chinese Key	C	C#	D	D#	E	F	F#	G	G#	A	A#	B
Western Key	C	D♭	D	E♭	E	F	F#	G	A♭	A	B♭	B

C KEY MODES (HUÁNG ZHŌNG Lǜ, 黄钟律)

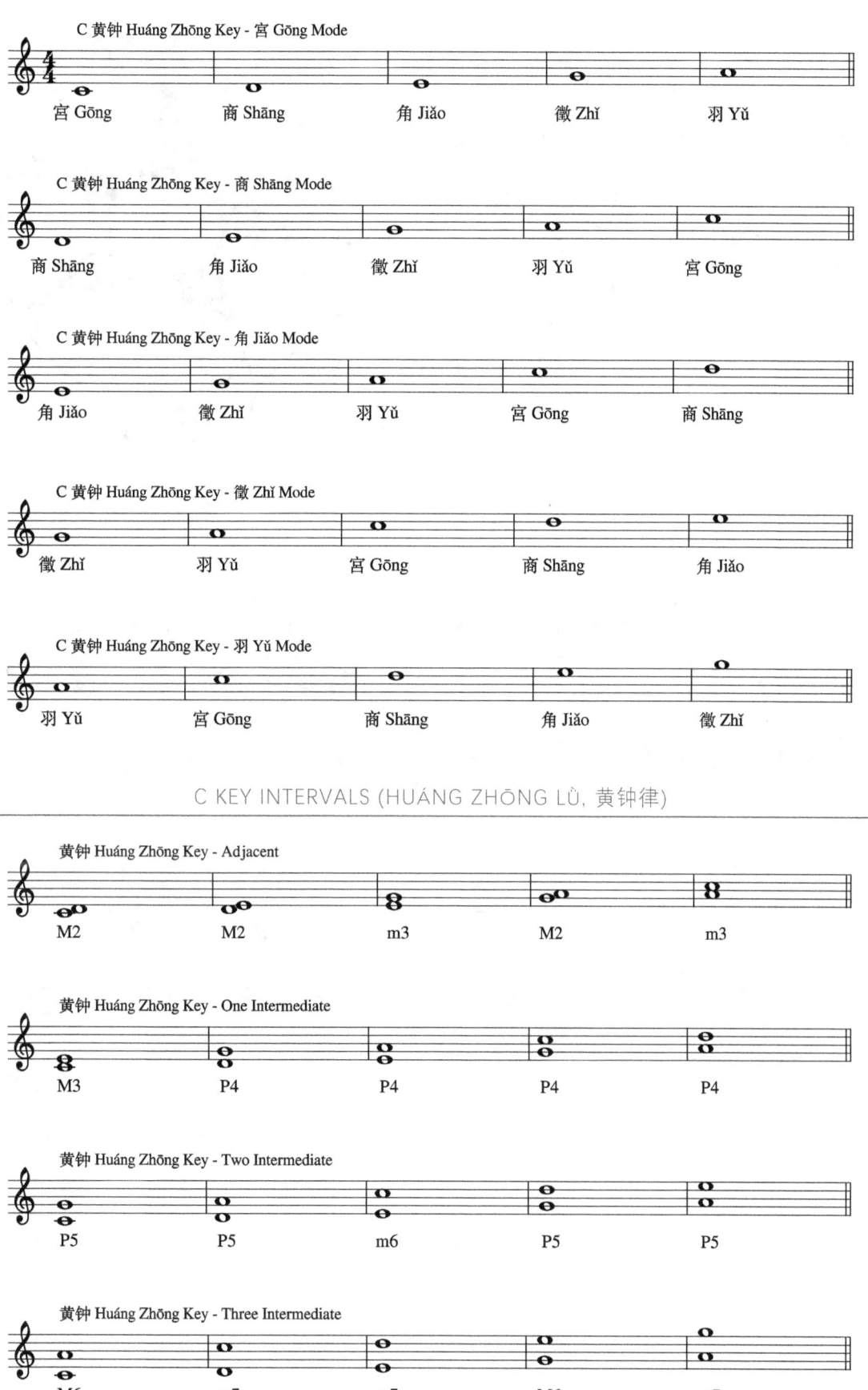

C KEY INTERVALS (HUÁNG ZHŌNG Lǜ, 黄钟律)

C KEY CHORDS (HUÁNG ZHŌNG Lǜ, 黄钟律)

Root		12 TET Chord		Pentatonic Chord	
宫	Gōng	C	I	C	IP
商	Shāng	Dm	ii	D5/7	iiP
角	Jiǎo	Em	iii	Em7	iiiP
徵	Zhǐ	G	V	G9	VP
羽	Yǔ	Am	vi	Am	vimP

TABLE 7 C KEY CHORDS

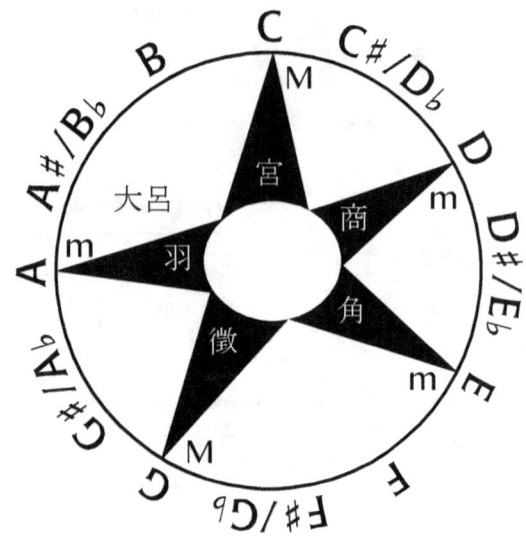

FIGURE 1 C KEY CHROMATIC CIRCLE

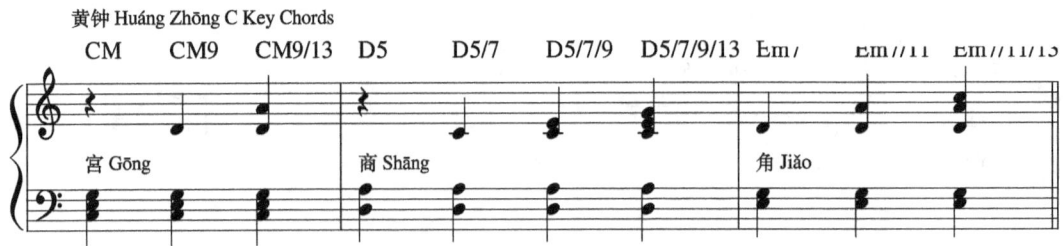

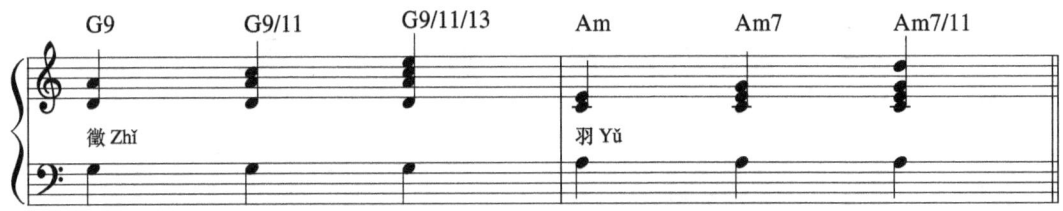

C KEY SCALES (HUÁNG ZHŌNG Lǜ, 黄钟律)

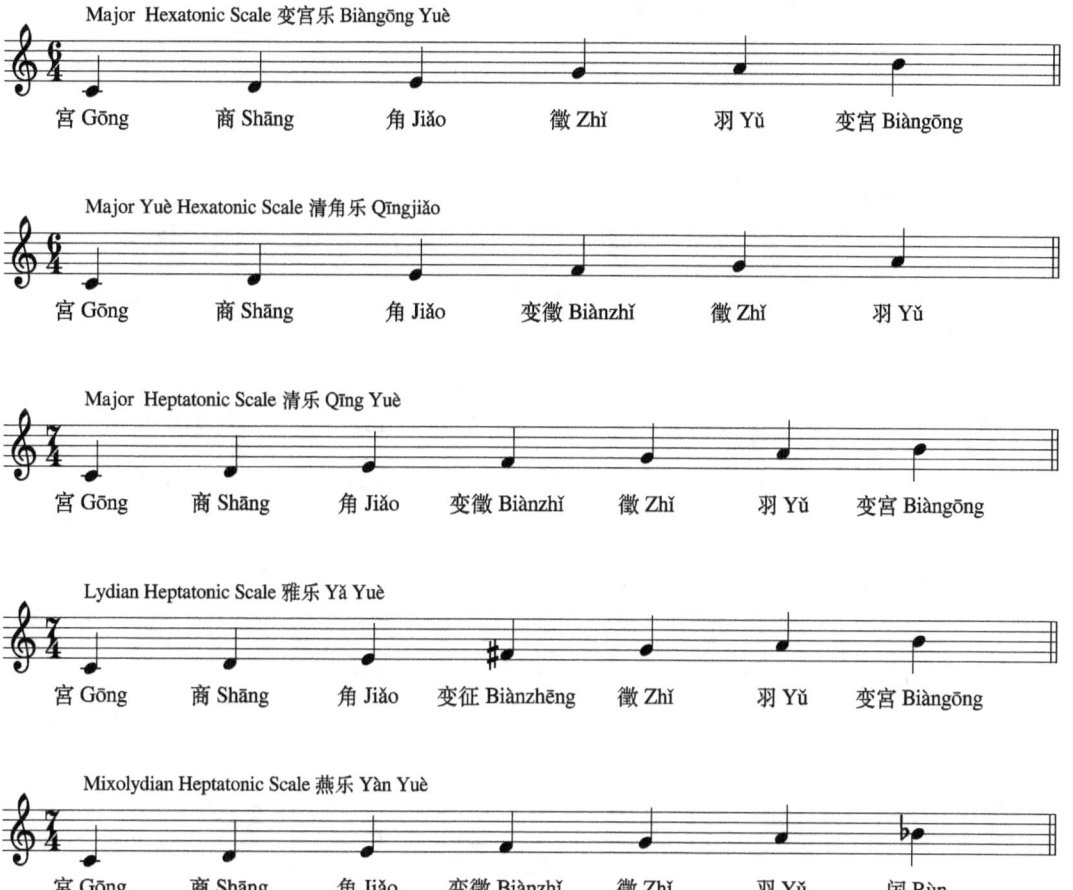

C# KEY MODES (DÀ LǙ LÜ, 大呂律)

C# KEY CHORDS (DÀ LǙ Lǜ, 大呂律)

Root		12 TET Chord		Pentatonic Chord	
宮	Gōng	C#	I	C#	IP
商	Shāng	D#m	ii	D#5/7	iiP
角	Jiǎo	Fm (E#m)	iii	Fm7no5 (E#m)	iiiP
徵	Zhǐ	G#	V	G#9	VP
羽	Yǔ	A#m	vi	A#m	vimP

TABLE 8 C# KEY CHORDS

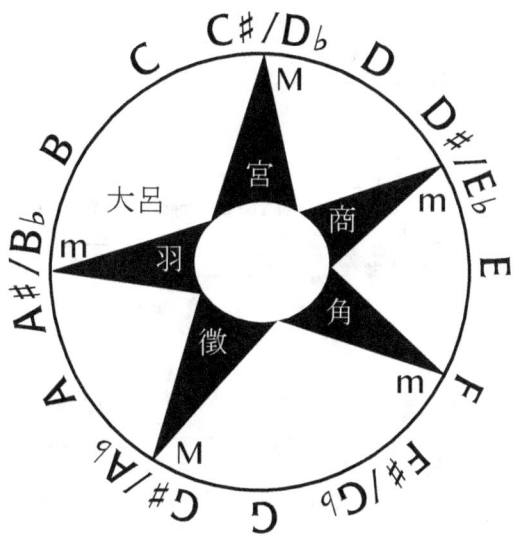

FIGURE 2 C# KEY CHROMATIC CIRCLE

C# KEY SCALES (DÀ LǙ LÙ, 大吕律)

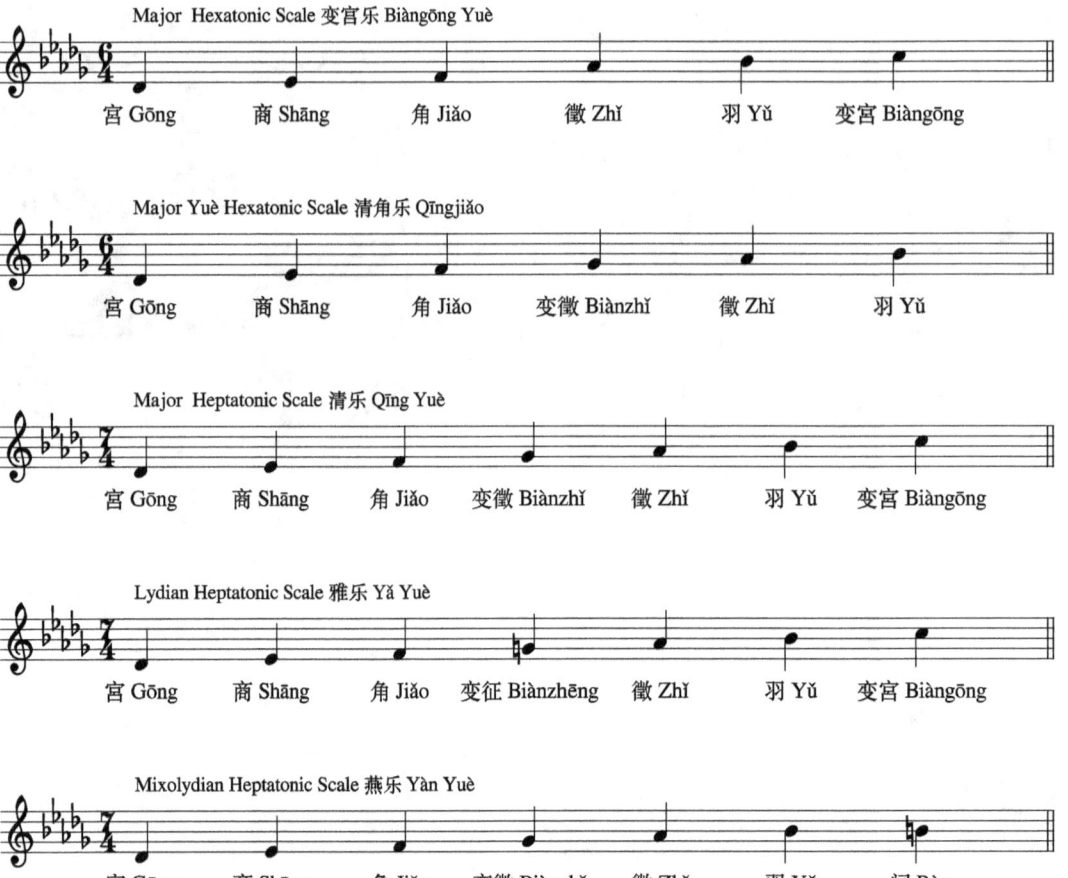

D KEY MODES (TÀI CÙ LÙ, 太簇 LÙ)

D KEY INTERVALS (TÀI CÙ LÙ, 太簇 LÙ)

D KEY CHORDS (TÀI CÙ LǛ, 太簇 LǛ)

Root		12 TET Chord		Pentatonic Chord	
宮	Gōng	D	I	D	IP
商	Shāng	Em	ii	Em5/7	iiP
角	Jiǎo	F#m	iii	F#m7no5	iiiP
徵	Zhǐ	A	V	A9	VP
羽	Yǔ	Bm	vi	Bm	viP

TABLE 9 D KEY CHORDS

FIGURE 3 D KEY CHROMATIC CIRCLE

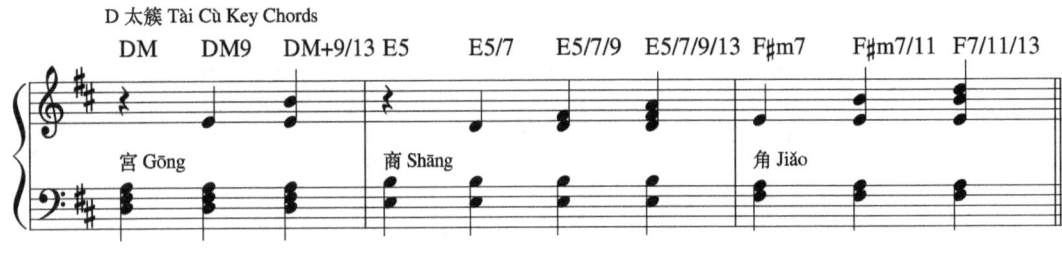

D KEY SCALES (TÀI CÙ LǛ, 太簇 LǛ)

D# KEY MODES (JIÁ ZHŌNG LǛ, 夹钟律)

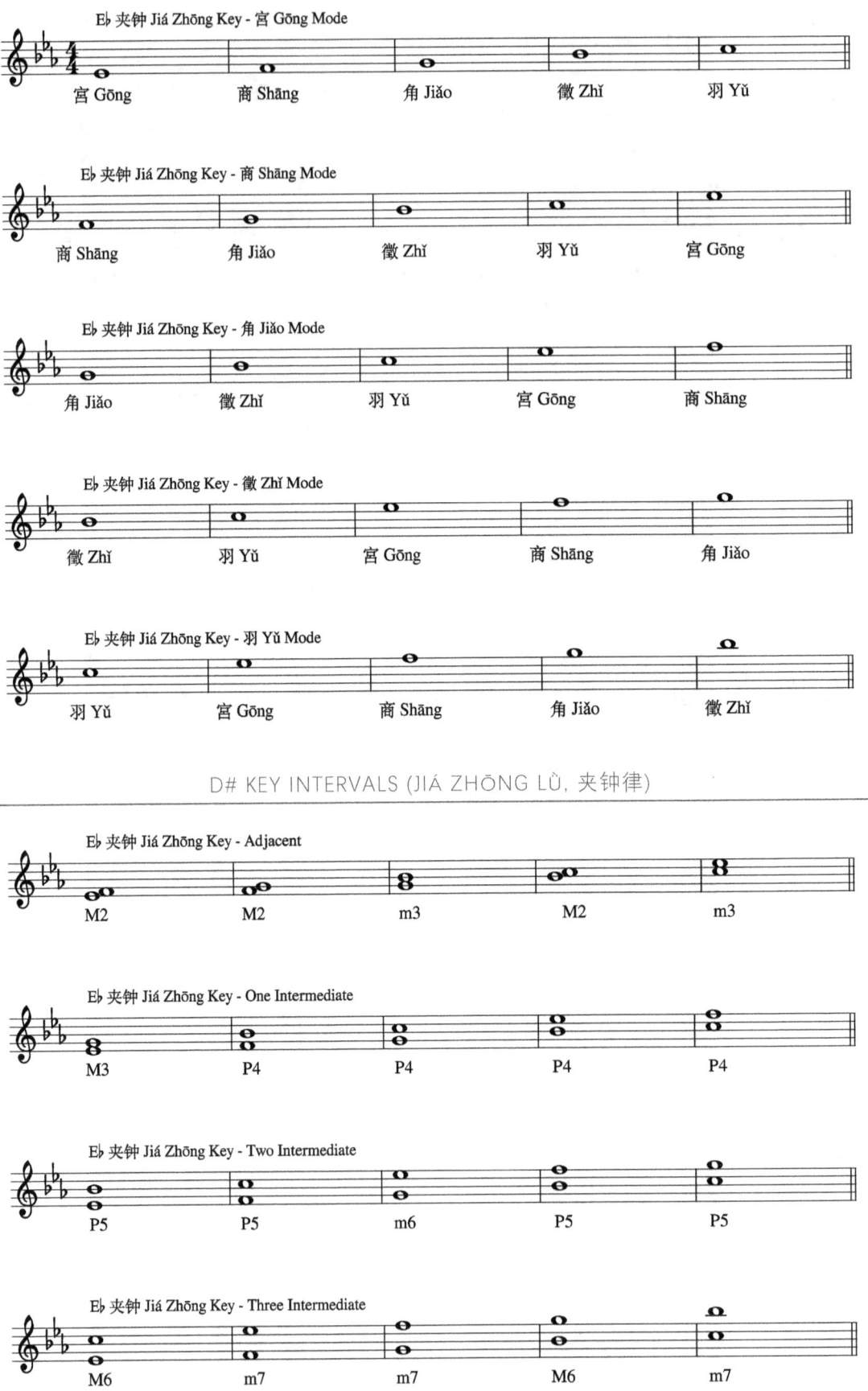

D# KEY INTERVALS (JIÁ ZHŌNG LǛ, 夹钟律)

D# KEY CHORDS (JIÁ ZHŌNG LǛ, 夹钟律)

	Root	12 TET Chord		Pentatonic Chord	
宫	Gōng	D#	I	D#	IP
商	Shāng	Fm	ii	Fm5/7	iiP
角	Jiǎo	Gm	iii	Gm7no5	iiiP
徵	Zhǐ	A#	V	A#9	VP
羽	Yǔ	Cm	vi	Cm	viP

TABLE 10 D# KEY CHORDS

FIGURE 4 D# KEY CHORMATIC CIRCLE

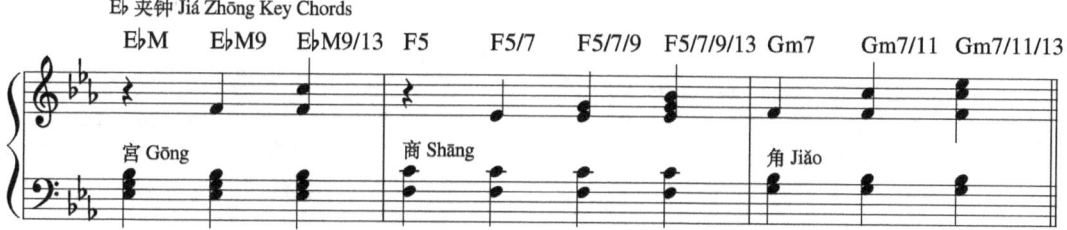

D# KEY SCALES (JIÁ ZHŌNG LǛ, 夹钟律)

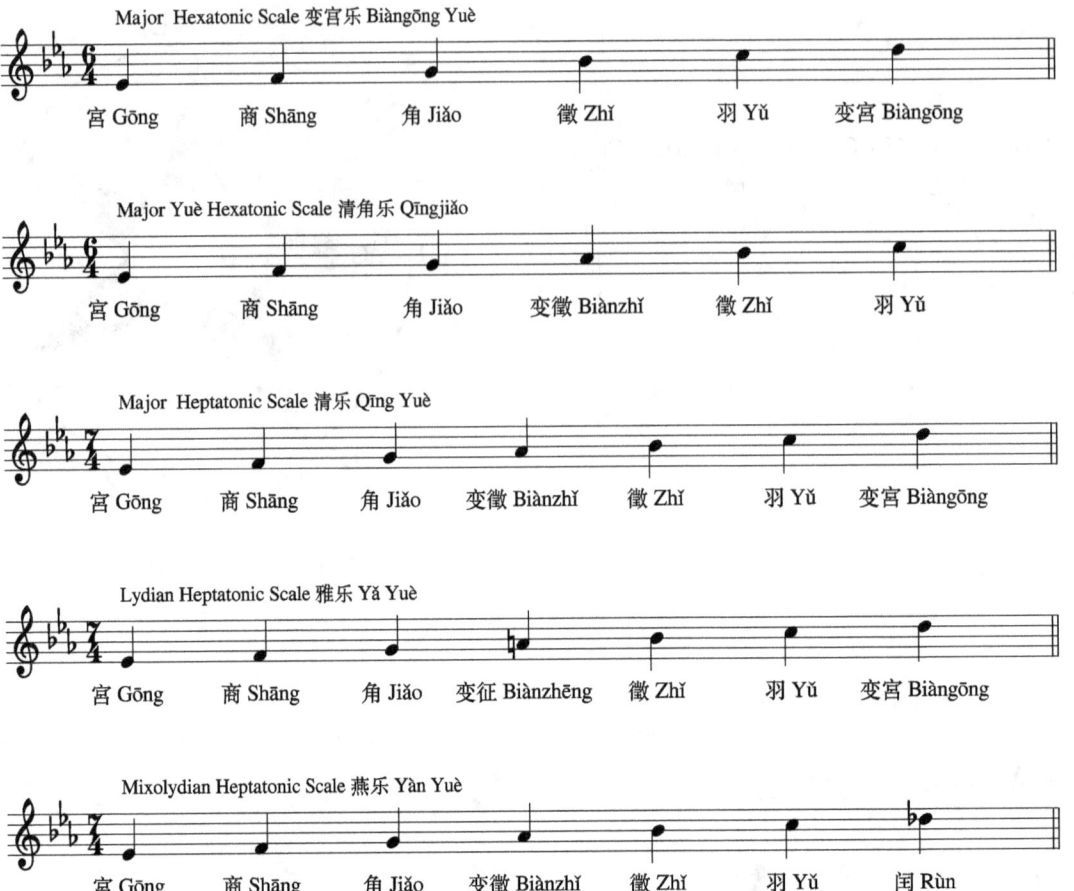

E KEY MODES (GŪ XIĂN LÜ, 姑洗律)

E KEY CHORDS (GŪ XIĂN LÜ, 姑洗律)

	Root	12 TET Chord		Pentatonic Chord	
宮	Gōng	E	I	E	IP
商	Shāng	F#m	ii	F#m5/7	iiP
角	Jiǎo	G#m	iii	G#m7no5	iiiP
徵	Zhǐ	B	V	B9	VP
羽	Yǔ	C#m	vi	C#m	vimP

TABLE 11 E KEY CHORDS

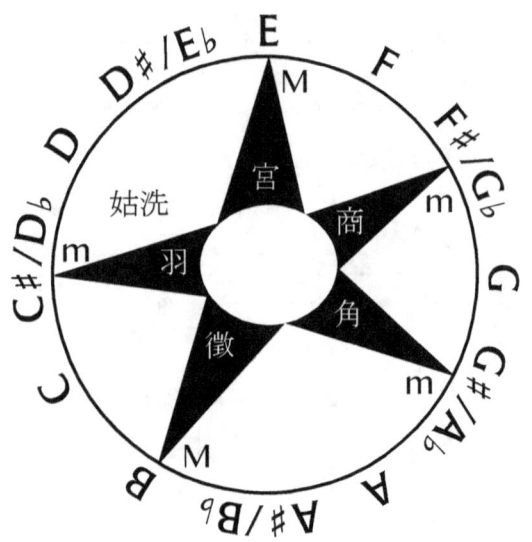

FIGURE 5 E KEY CHORMATIC CIRCLE

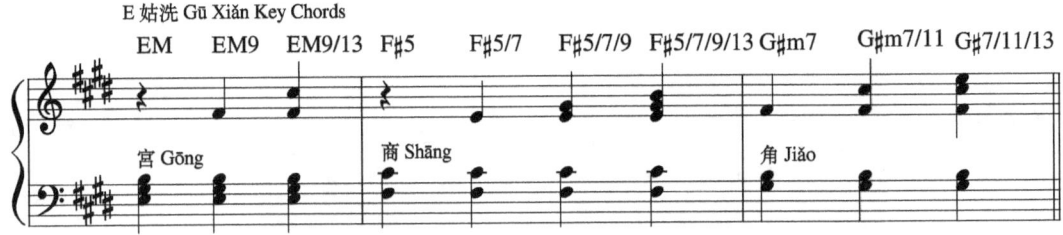

E KEY SCALES (GŪ XIĂN LǛ, 姑洗律)

F KEY MODES (ZHÒNG LǓ LÙ, 仲呂律)

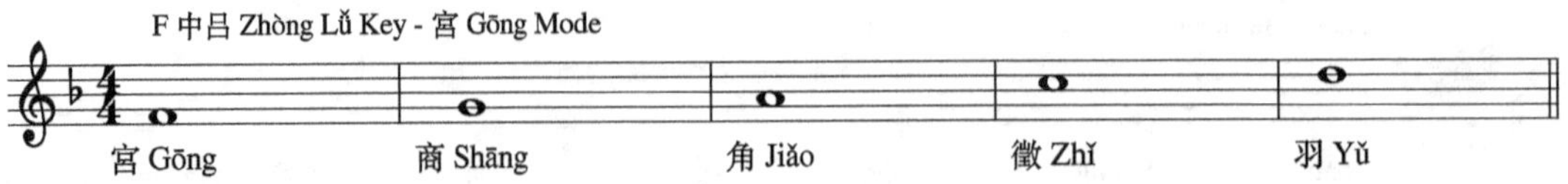

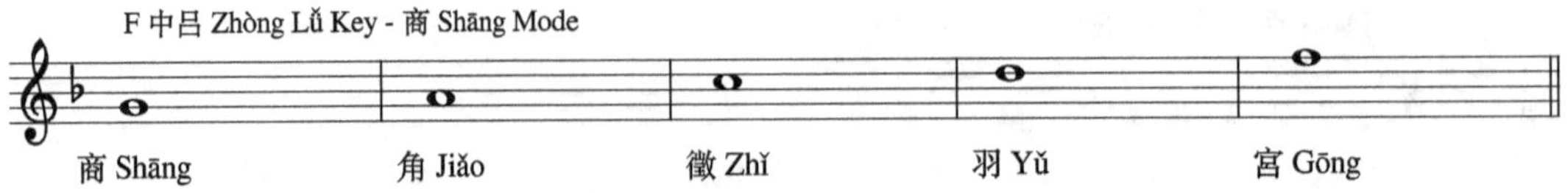

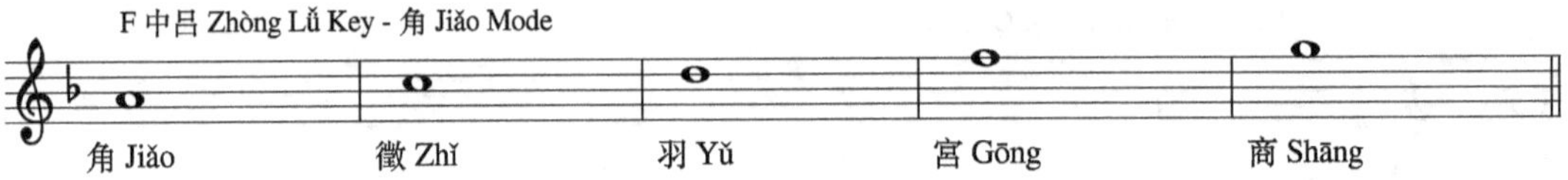

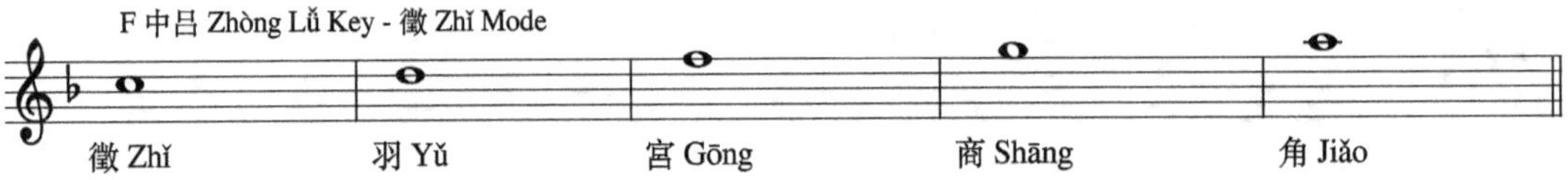

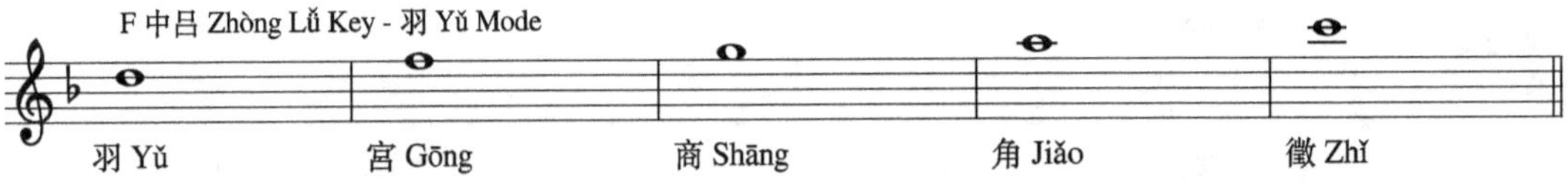

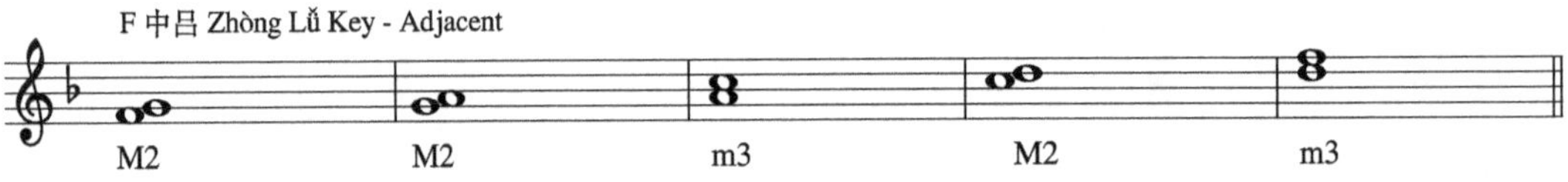

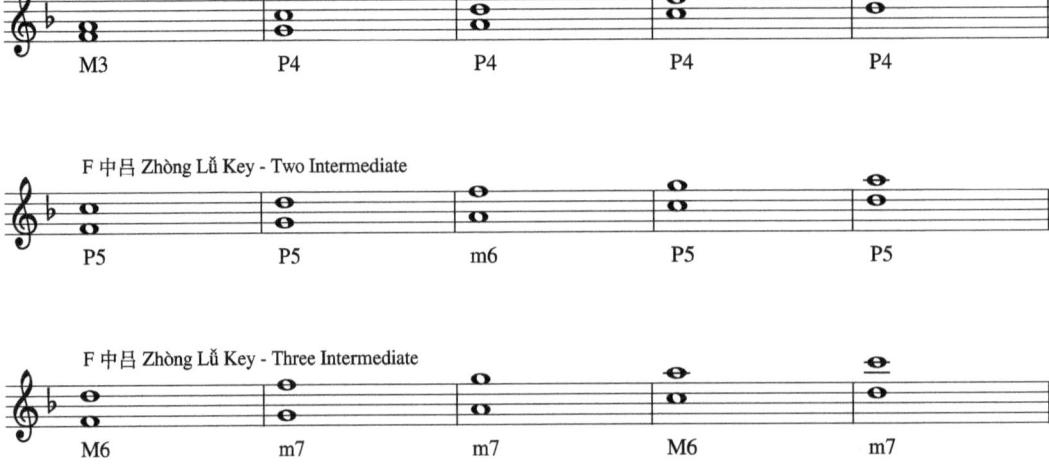

F KEY CHORDS (ZHÒNG LǙ LǛ, 仲吕律)

Root		12 TET Chord		Pentatonic Chord	
宫	Gōng	F	I	F	IP
商	Shāng	Gm	ii	Gm5/7	iiP
角	Jiǎo	Am	iii	Am7no5	iiiP
徵	Zhǐ	C	V	C9	VP
羽	Yǔ	Dm	vi	Dm	vimP

TABLE 12 F KEY CHORDS

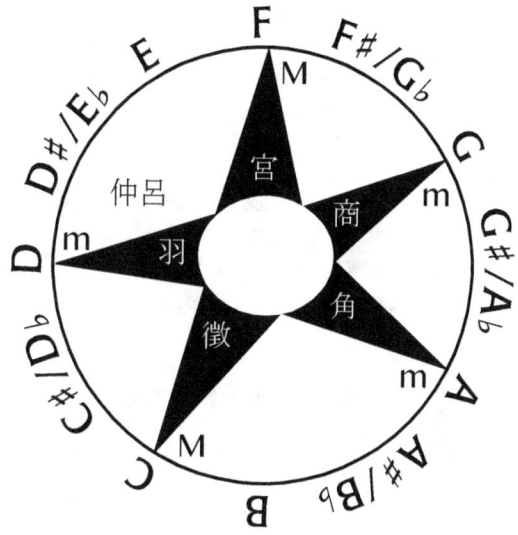

FIGURE 6 F KEY CHORMATIC CIRCLE

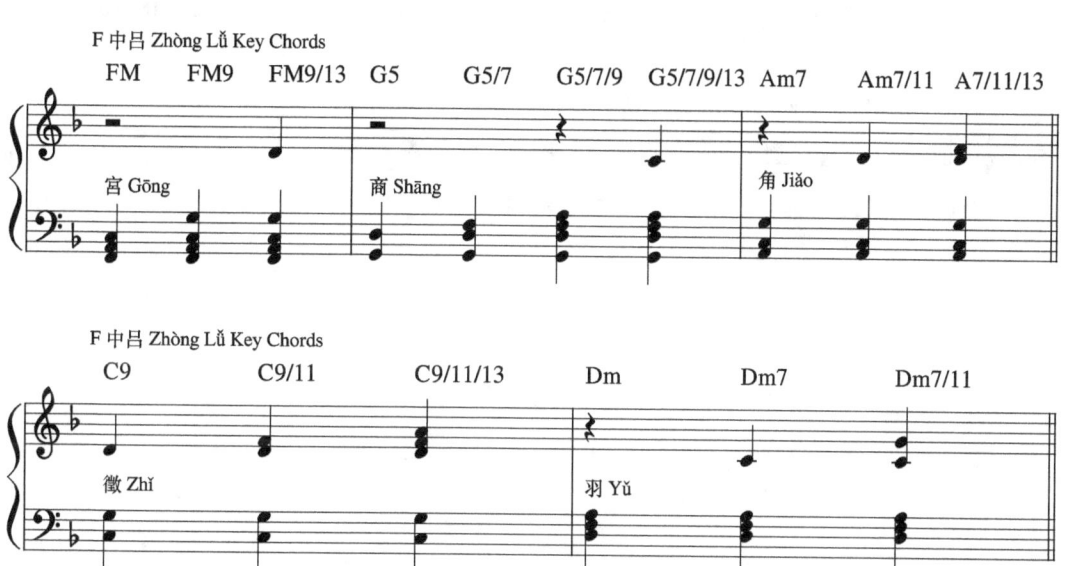

F KEY SCALES (ZHÒNG LǛ LǛ, 仲吕律)

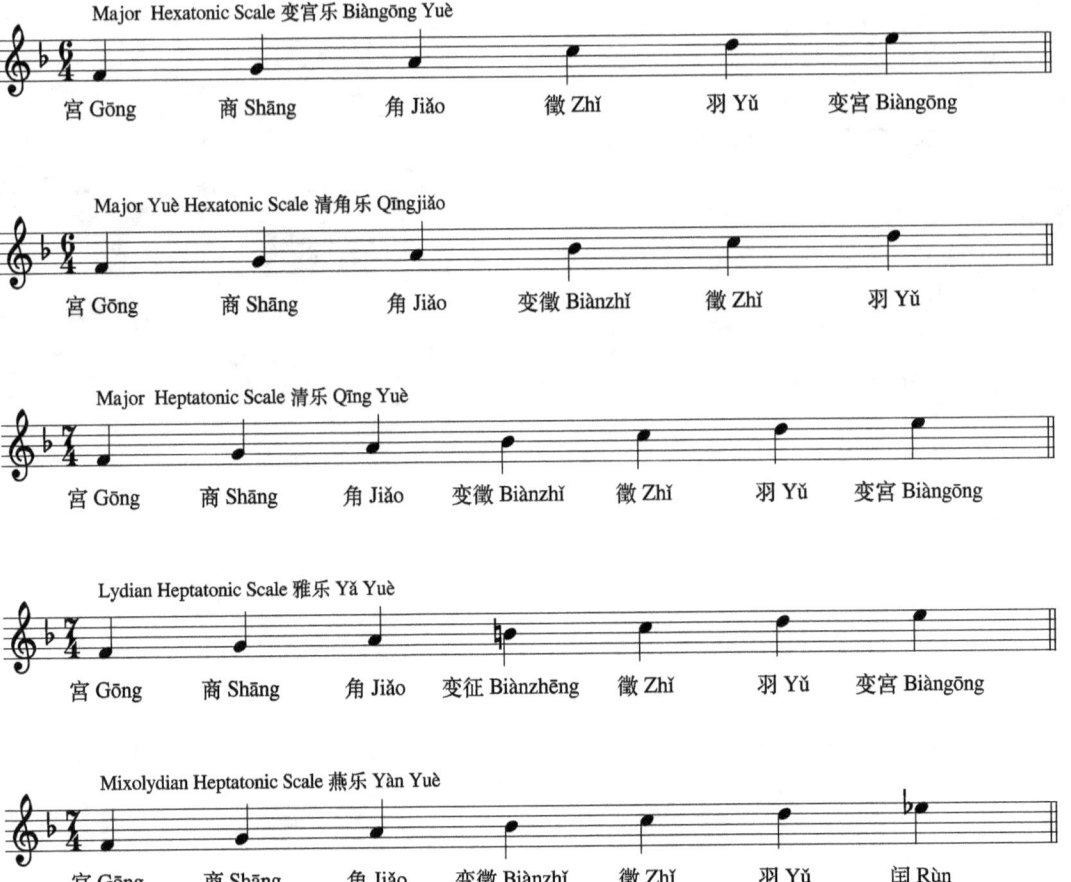

F# KEY MODES (RUÍ BĪN LǛ, 蕤宾律)

F# KEY INERVALS (RUÍ BĪN LǛ, 蕤宾律)

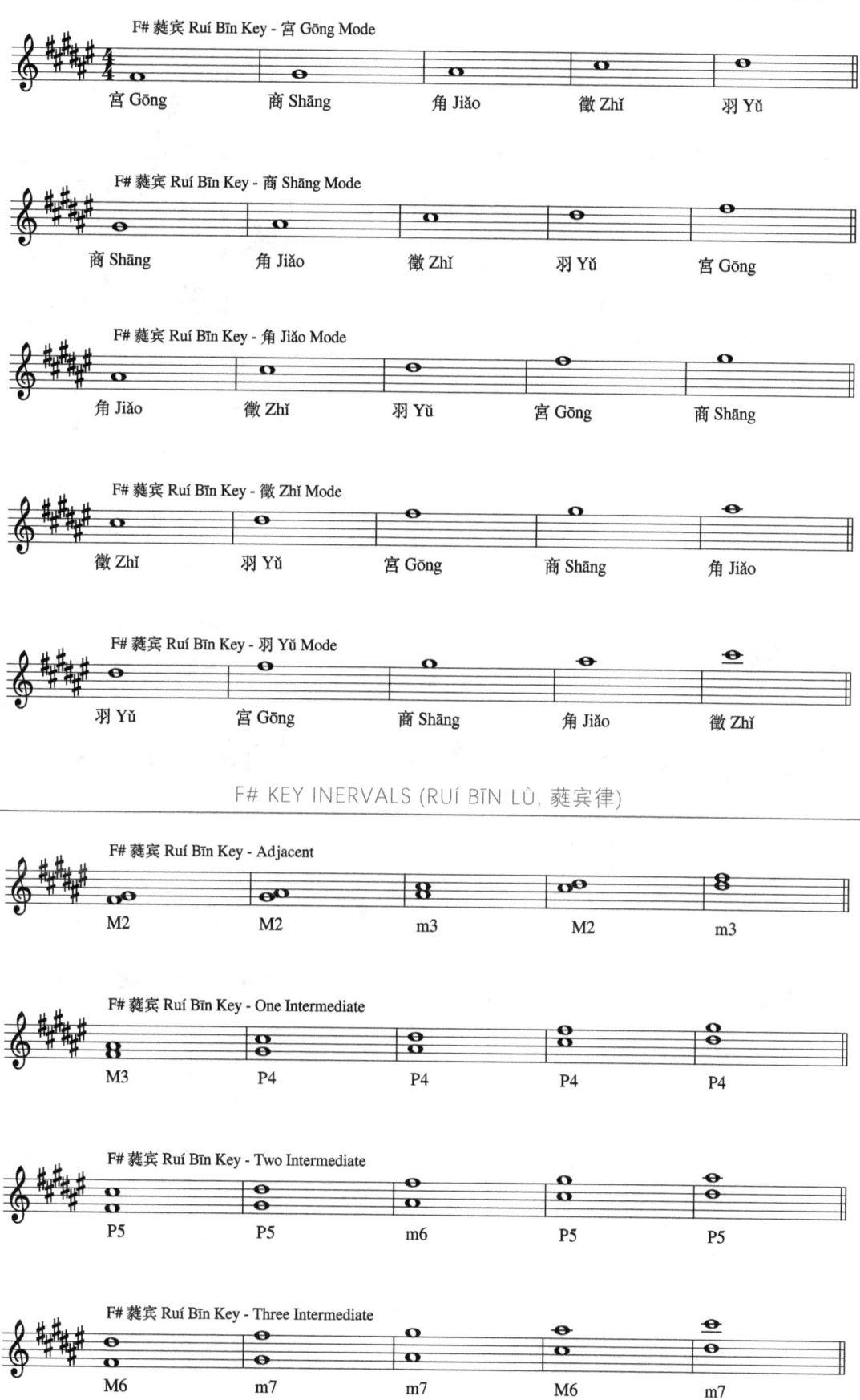

F# KEY CHORDS (RUÍ BĪN LÙ, 蕤宾律)

	Root	12 TET Chord		Pentatonic Chord	
宫	Gōng	F#	I	F#	IP
商	Shāng	G#m	ii	G#m5/7	iiP
角	Jiǎo	A#m	iii	A#m7no5	iiiP
徵	Zhǐ	C#	V	C#9	VP
羽	Yǔ	D#m	vi	D#m	vimP

TABLE 13 F# KEY CHORDS

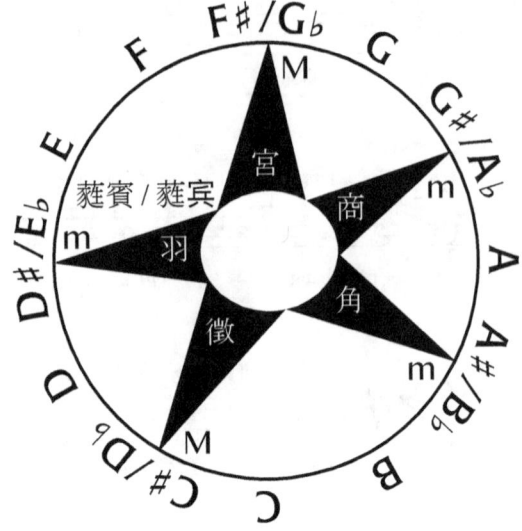

FIGURE 7 F# KEY CHORMATIC CIRCLE

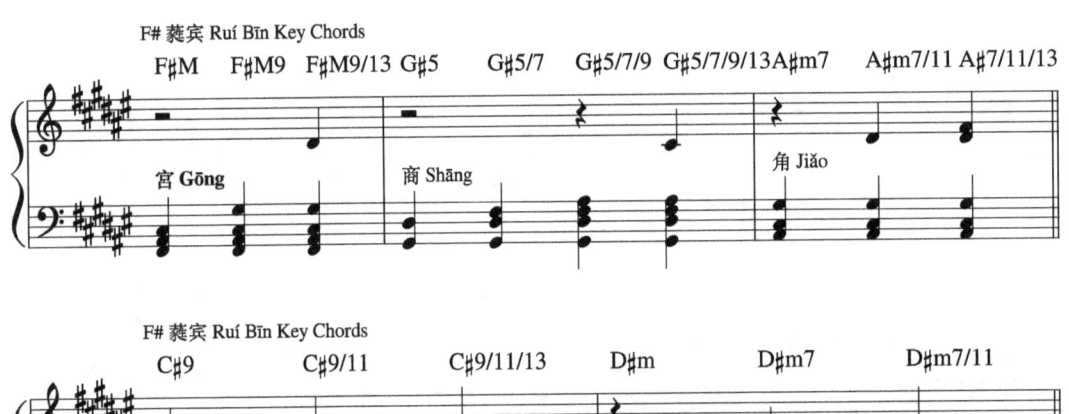

F# KEY SCALES (RUÍ BĪN LÜ, 蕤宾律)

G KEY MODES (LÍN ZHŌNG LǙ, 林钟律)

G KEY INTERVALS (LÍN ZHŌNG LǙ, 林钟律)

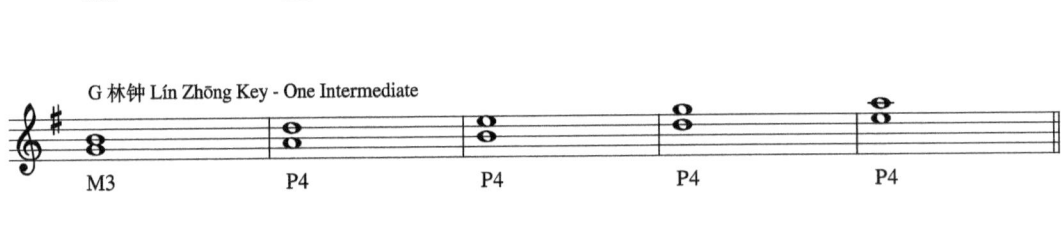
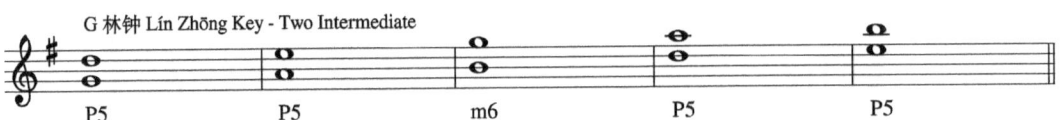
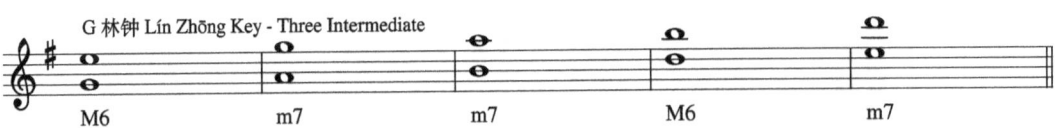

G KEY CHORDS (LÍN ZHŌNG LǛ, 林钟律)

	Root	12 TET Chord		Pentatonic Chord	
宫	Gōng	G	I	G	IP
商	Shāng	Am	ii	Am5/7	iiP
角	Jiǎo	Bm	iii	Bm7no5	iiiP
徵	Zhǐ	D	V	D9	VP
羽	Yǔ	Em	vi	Em	vimP

TABLE 14 G KEY CHORDS

FIGURE 8 G KEY CHORMATIC CIRCLE

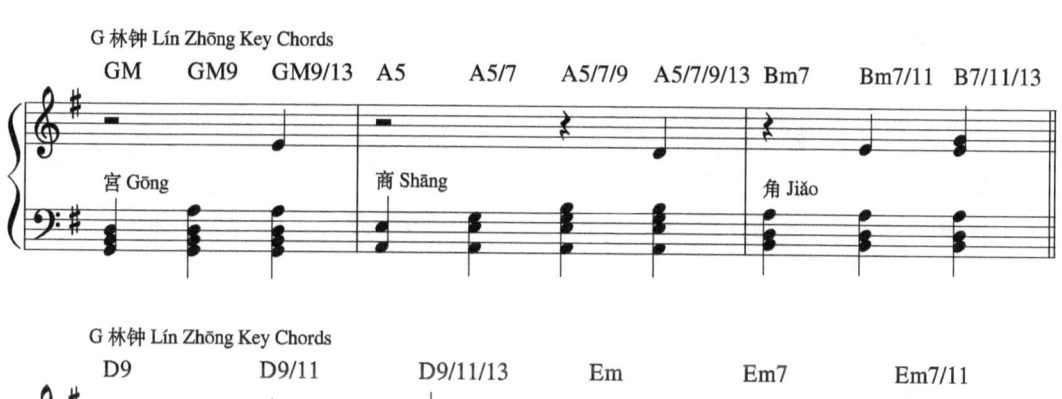

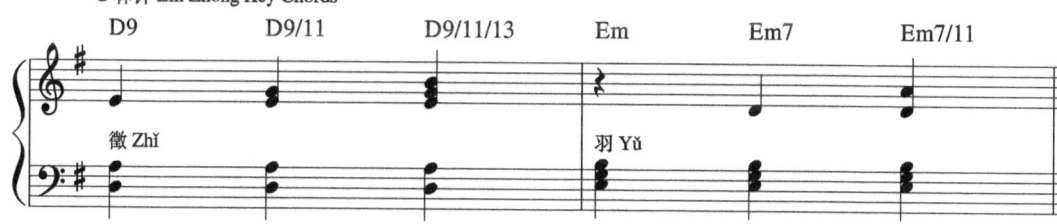

G# KEY MODES (Yí Zé Lǜ, 夷則律)

G# KEY INTERVALS (Yí Zé Lǜ, 夷則律)

G# KEY CHORDS (Yí Zé Lǜ, 夷則律)

Root		12 TET Chord		Pentatonic Chord	
宮	Gōng	G#	I	G#	IP
商	Shāng	A#m	ii	A#m5/7	iiP
角	Jiǎo	Cm	iii	Cm7no5	iiiP
徵	Zhǐ	D#	V	D#9	VP
羽	Yǔ	Fm	vi	Fm	vimP

TABLE 15 G# KEY CHORDS

FIGURE 9 G# KEY CHORMATIC CIRCLE

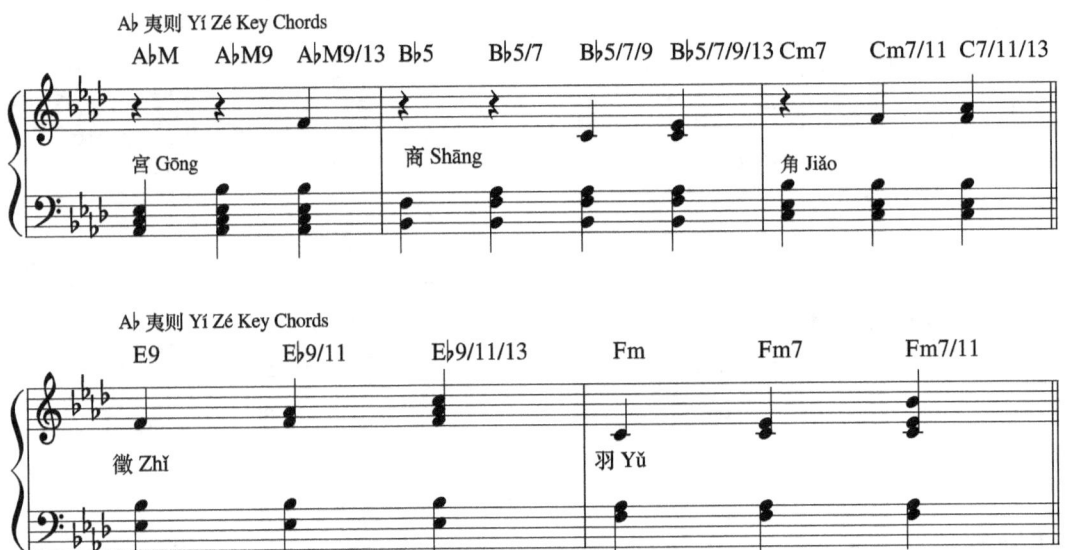

G# KEY SCALES (YÍ ZÉ LÜ, 夷則律)

A KEY MODES (NÁN LǙ LÙ, 南呂律)

A KEY INTERVALS (NÁN LǙ LÙ, 南呂律)

A KEY CHORDS (NÁN LǙ LǛ, 南呂律)

Root		12 TET Chord		Pentatonic Chord	
宮	Gōng	A	I	A	IP
商	Shāng	Bm	ii	Bm5/7	iiP
角	Jiǎo	C#m	iii	C#m7no5	iiiP
徵	Zhǐ	E	V	E9	VP
羽	Yǔ	F#m	vi	F#m	vimP

TABLE 16 A KEY CHORDS

FIGURE 10 A KEY CHORMATIC CIRCLE

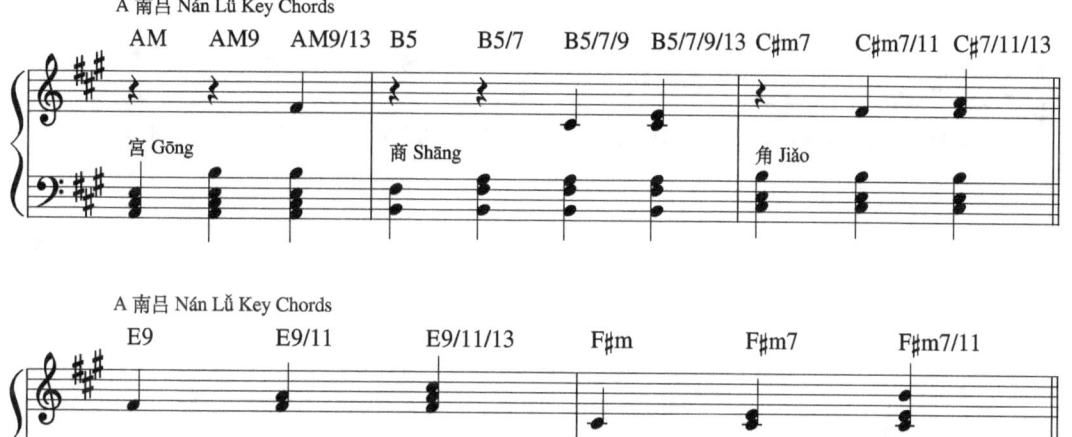

A KEY SCALES (NÁN LǙ LÜ, 南吕律)

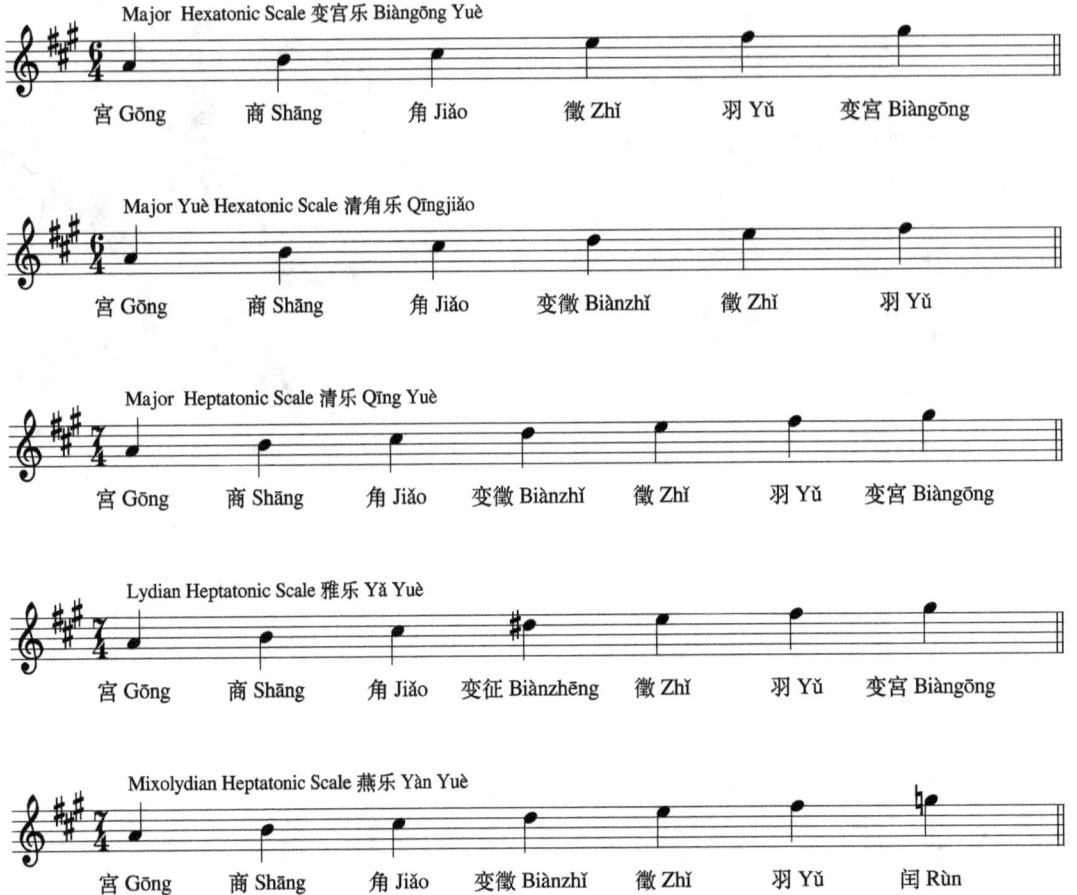

A# KEY MODES (WÚ YÌ LǙ, 无射 LǙ)

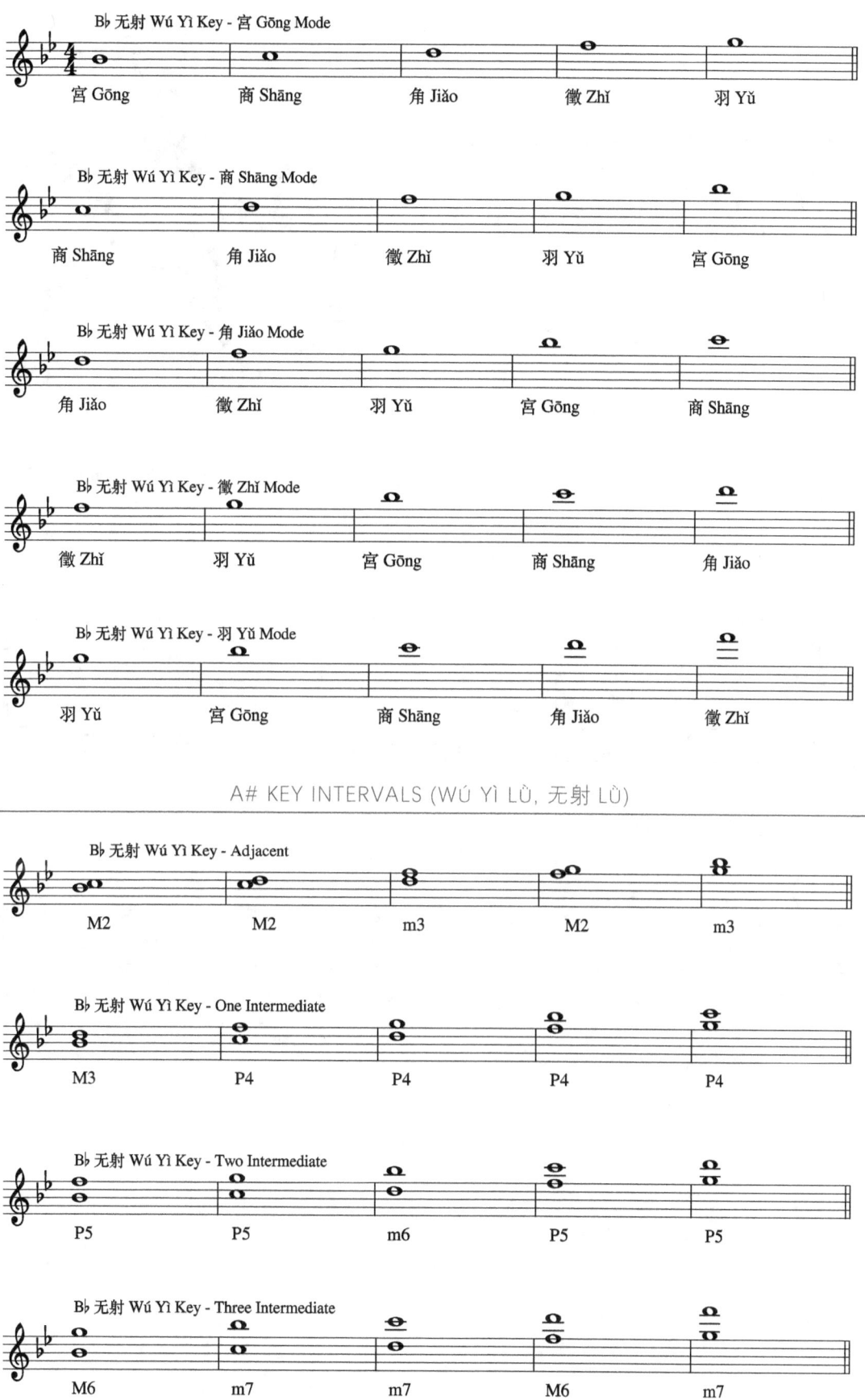

A# KEY INTERVALS (WÚ YÌ LǙ, 无射 LǙ)

A# KEY CHORDS (WÚ YÌ LÜ, 无射 LÜ)

Root		12 TET Chord		Pentatonic Chord	
宫	Gōng	A#	I	A#	IP
商	Shāng	Cm	ii	Cm5/7	iiP
角	Jiǎo	Dm	iii	Dm7no5	iiiP
徵	Zhǐ	F	V	F9	VP
羽	Yǔ	Gm	vi	Gm	vimP

TABLE 17 A# KEY CHORDS

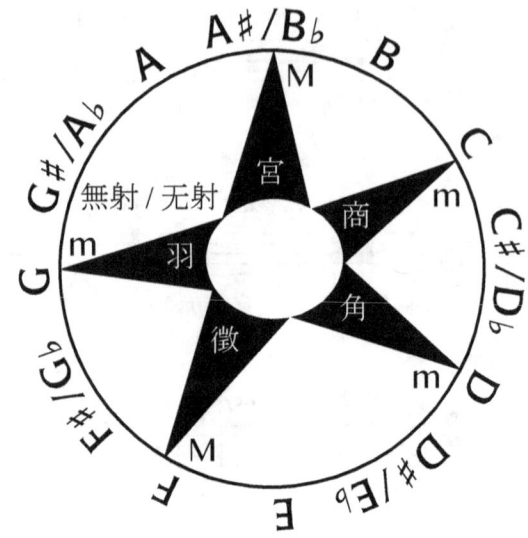

FIGURE 11 A# KEY CHORMATIC CIRCLE

A# KEY SCALES (WÚ YÌ LÙ, 无射 LÙ)

B KEY MODES (YÌNG ZHŌNG LǛ, 应钟律)

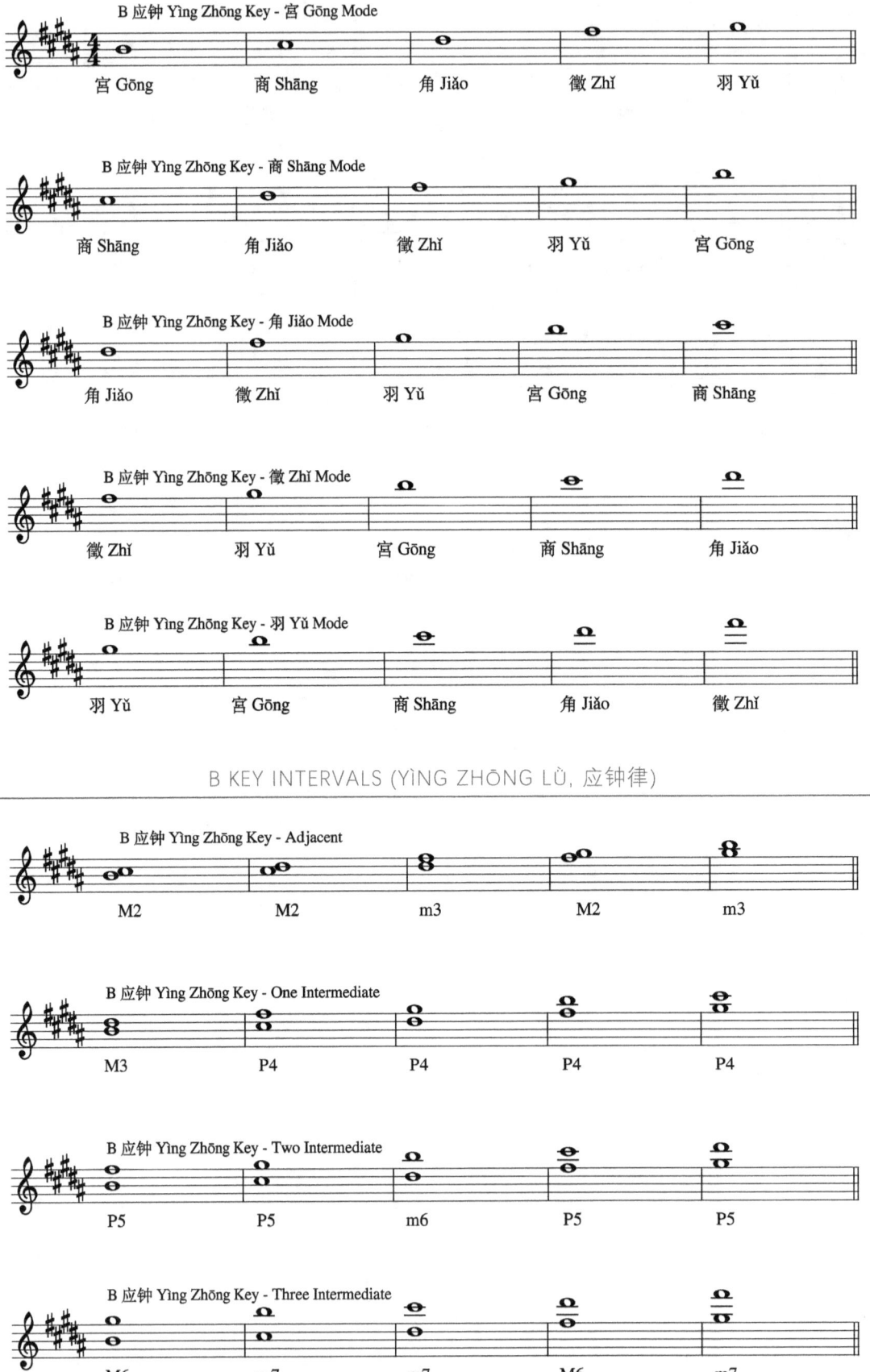

B KEY CHORDS (YÌNG ZHŌNG Lǜ, 应钟律)

	Root	12 TET Chord		Pentatonic Chord	
宫	Gōng	B	I	B	IP
商	Shāng	C#m	ii	C#m5/7	iiP
角	Jiǎo	D#m	iii	D#m7no5	iiiP
徵	Zhǐ	F#	V	F#9	VP
羽	Yǔ	G#m	vi	G#m	vimP

TABLE 18 B KEY CHORDS

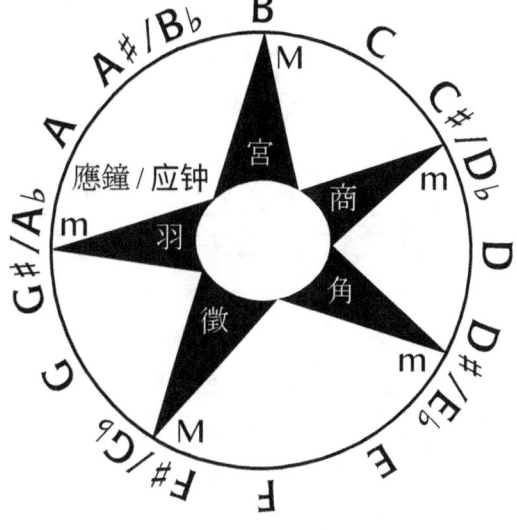

FIGURE 12 B KEY CHORMATIC CIRCLE

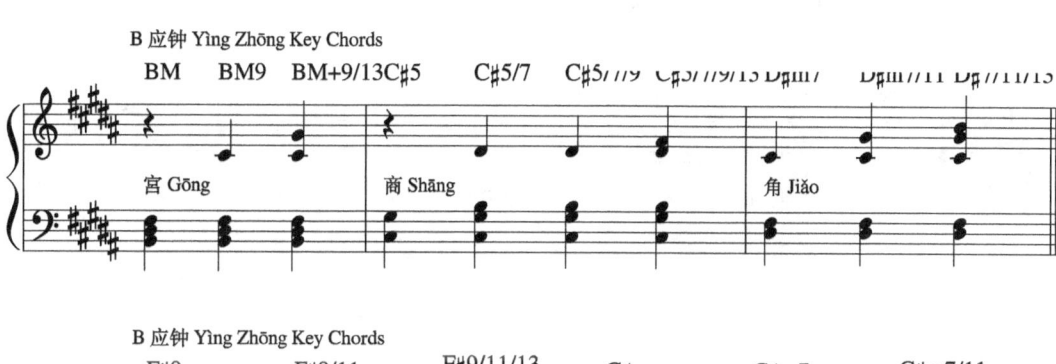

B KEY SCALES (YÌNG ZHŌNG LÜ, 应钟律)

PROGRESSIONS

2 NOTE SCALE PROGRESSIONS

3 NOTE SCALE PROGRESSIONS

4 NOTE SCALE PROGRESSIONS

5 NOTE SCALE PROGRESSIONS

HARMONY

Sometimes Chinese Music is described as melody and percussion. It makes little use of harmony. Ambience and musical cues are not provided by harmony, they are provided by the percussion section. See Percussion for more on this topic.

Where harmony does exist, the harmony is normally provided by a Support Voice (Zhī Shēng Xíng, 支聲型). This Support Voice cannot vary too far from the main melody and moves in close intervals. Major Pentatonic Two-part Harmony commonly uses the note intervals of a Minor Third, Perfect Fourth, and Perfect Fifth. Parallel movement is common but non-parallel and contrary motion are also used.

Within the various regional types of Chinese Music different intervals are more common. Also, standard resolutions are subject to regional variation.

Within the different modes some notes are considered stable, and some are unstable. Harmonies are generally based on the stable notes.

	Harmonic Mode	Stable Notes	Unstable Notes
宮调	Gōngdiào	1, 3, 5	6, 2
商调	Shāngdiào	2, 5, 6	1, 3
角调	Jiǎodiào	3, 5, 6	1, 2
徵调	Zhǐdiào	5, 1, 2	3, 6
羽调	Yǔdiào	6, 1, 2, 3	5

TABLE 19 HARMONIC NOTES

1 2 3 5 6   2 3 5 6 .1   3 5 6 .1 .2   5 6 .1 .2 .3   6 .1 .2 .3 .5

SWITCHING KEYS

In some texts the five Positive Modes are shown using the same starting note. This means that the modes are in different keys. This is a good way of switching keys.

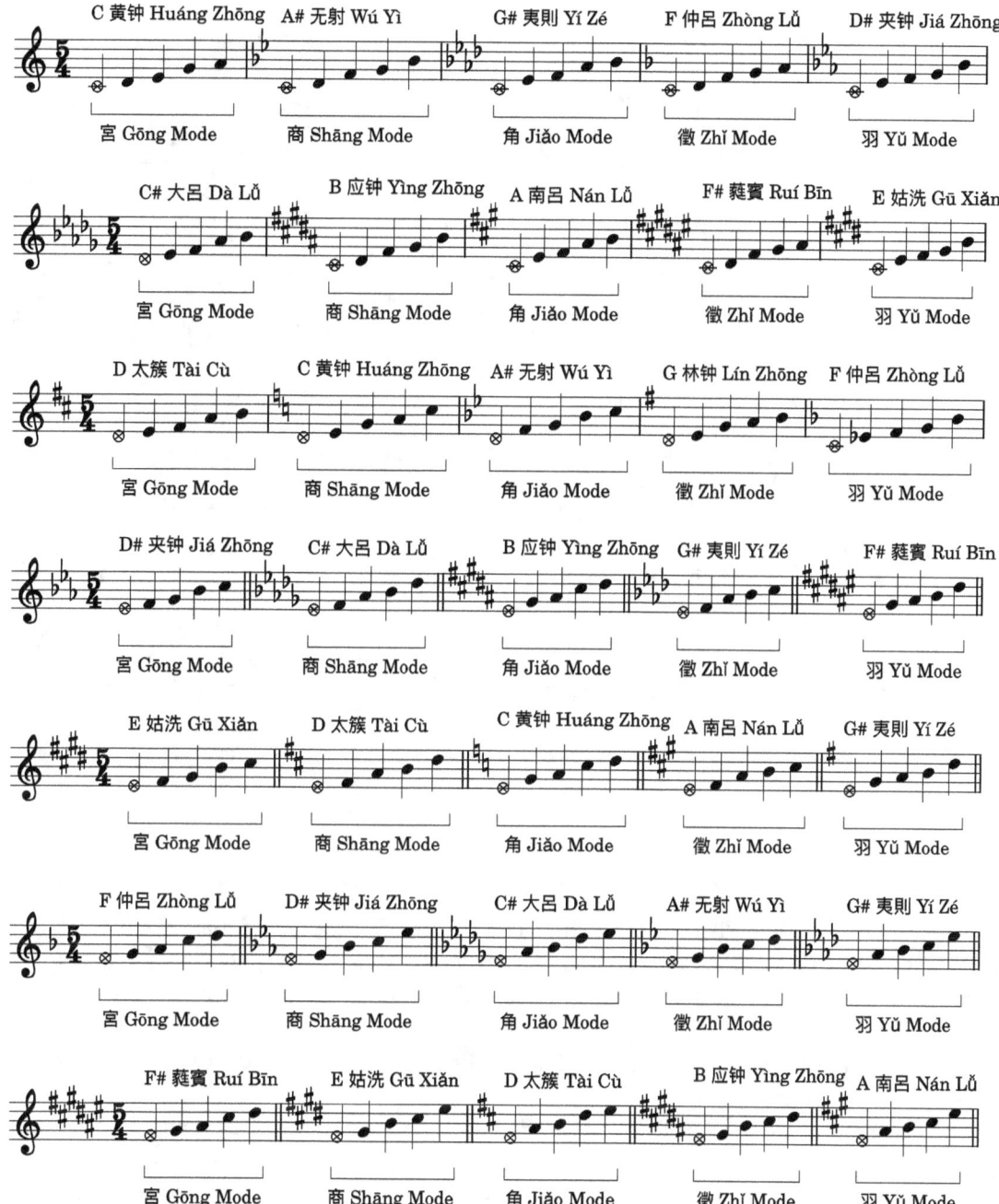

BEAT AND TIME (PĀI, 拍)

There are five types of Meter (Bǎnshì, 板式). The first four have Strict Time (Yǒubǎn, 有板). The fifth is Free Meter (Sǎnbǎn, 散板). While I have only shown the standard times: 1/4, 2/4, 4/4, and 8/4, it is quite common to find bars of other lengths such as 3/4, and 5/4 in tunes.

There are two types of beat. There are strong Bǎn (板) beats, and weak Yǎn (眼) beats.

Note that in some sources the Bǎn (板) beats are fast and short, and the Yǎn (眼) beats are slow and long. If this were literally the case the timings would be very different. If we assume a 2:1 ratio between the length of the fast Yǎn (眼) beats and the slow Bǎn (板) beats then the timings in the following table would be: 1/8, 3/8, 7/8, and 15/8 respectively.

	Name	Time	Strong Beats	Weak Beats	Tempo
快板	Kuàibǎn	$\frac{1}{4}$	1	0	Fast - Allegro
中板	Zhōngbǎn	$\frac{2}{4}$	1	1	Moderate - Moderato
慢板	Mànbǎn	$\frac{4}{4}$	1	3	Moderate - Adagio

	Name	Time	Strong Beats	Weak Beats	Tempo
缓板	Huǎnbǎn	$\frac{8}{4}$	1	7	Slow – Lento or Largo
散板	Sǎnbǎn		Freely or irregular		Senza Misura
由板	Yóubǎn				
摇板	Yáobǎn		Syncopated or Shaking Beat		

TABLE 20 BEAT AND TEMPO

A Liúshuǐbǎn (流水板) is a fast and continuous rhythmic pattern.

Shuāngjiàn (双键) is typically used for double sword action. Two non-identical beats oscillate in a manner that shows harmony and coordination.

To create variety, or to speed up or slow down a rhythm, bars can be omitted, contracted, expanded or repeated.

To make a bar longer and slow down the music, one or more weak Yǎn (眼) beats can be added. For example: Adding a Yǎn (眼) to every Bǎn (板) can be used to double the length of a song that only includes Bǎn (板) beats.

A tune can be doubled in length by adding extra Yǎn (眼) beats every second beat even if the beat is already a Yǎn (眼) beat. This process is called Kuòbǎn (扩板). A more specific term Zēngbǎn (增板) is applied when changing a tune that is in 4/4 meter to 8/4 meter.

To make a bar, and hence the whole tune shorter, beats can be removed. This is called Subtracting Characters (Jiǎnzì, 减字).

A tune can also be made shorter by removing half the notes. This process is called Removing Unaccented Beats[8] (Chōuyǎn, 抽眼).

See the section on Tone Groups on page 63 for examples of adding and removing characters.

BEAT GROUPINGS (节拍组, JIÉPĀI ZǓ)

The Melody (Qǔdiào, 曲调) is made up of sets of phrases also known as beat groups. A typical tune may have eight phrases. These phrases or beat groups come in 8 or 12 beat lengths and are grouped into tone groups. A tone group is synonymous to the western concept of a bar. Unlike standard western

---

[8] Available sources are ambiguous in relation to which half of the notes are removed. As far as I can ascertain, it is valid to just use musical judgement as to which notes to remove. The purpose is to make the standard tune fit your needs.

music, which generally maintains only one or at most, a few time signatures within a single melody, it is normal for Chinese music to constantly change time signatures.

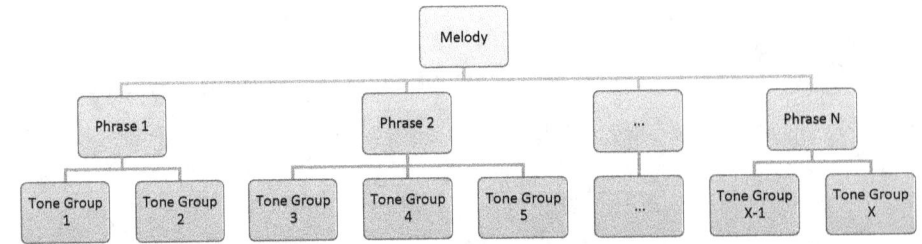

PHRASE LENGTH 8 – GROUPING 2+2+2+2

PHRASE LENGTH 8 – GROUPING 2+2+4

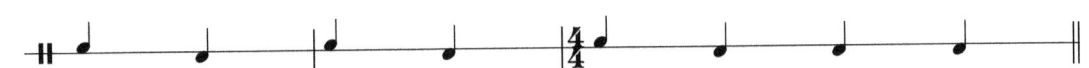

PHRASE LENGTH 8 – GROUPING 2+3+3

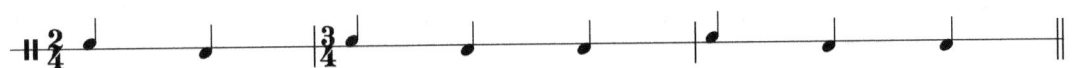

PHRASE LENGTH 8 – GROUPING 2+4+2

PHRASE LENGTH 8 – GROUPING 2+6

PHRASE LENGTH 8 – GROUPING 3+2+3

PHRASE LENGTH 8 – GROUPING 3+3+2

PHRASE LENGTH 8 – GROUPING 3+5

PHRASE LENGTH 8 – GROUPING 4+4

PHRASE LENGTH 8 – GROUPING 5+3

PHRASE LENGTH 8 – GROUPING 6+2

PHRASE LENGTH 12 – GROUPING 2+2+2+2+2+2

PHRASE LENGTH 12 – GROUPING +2+2+2+3+3

PHRASE LENGTH 12 – GROUPING +2+2+3+2+3

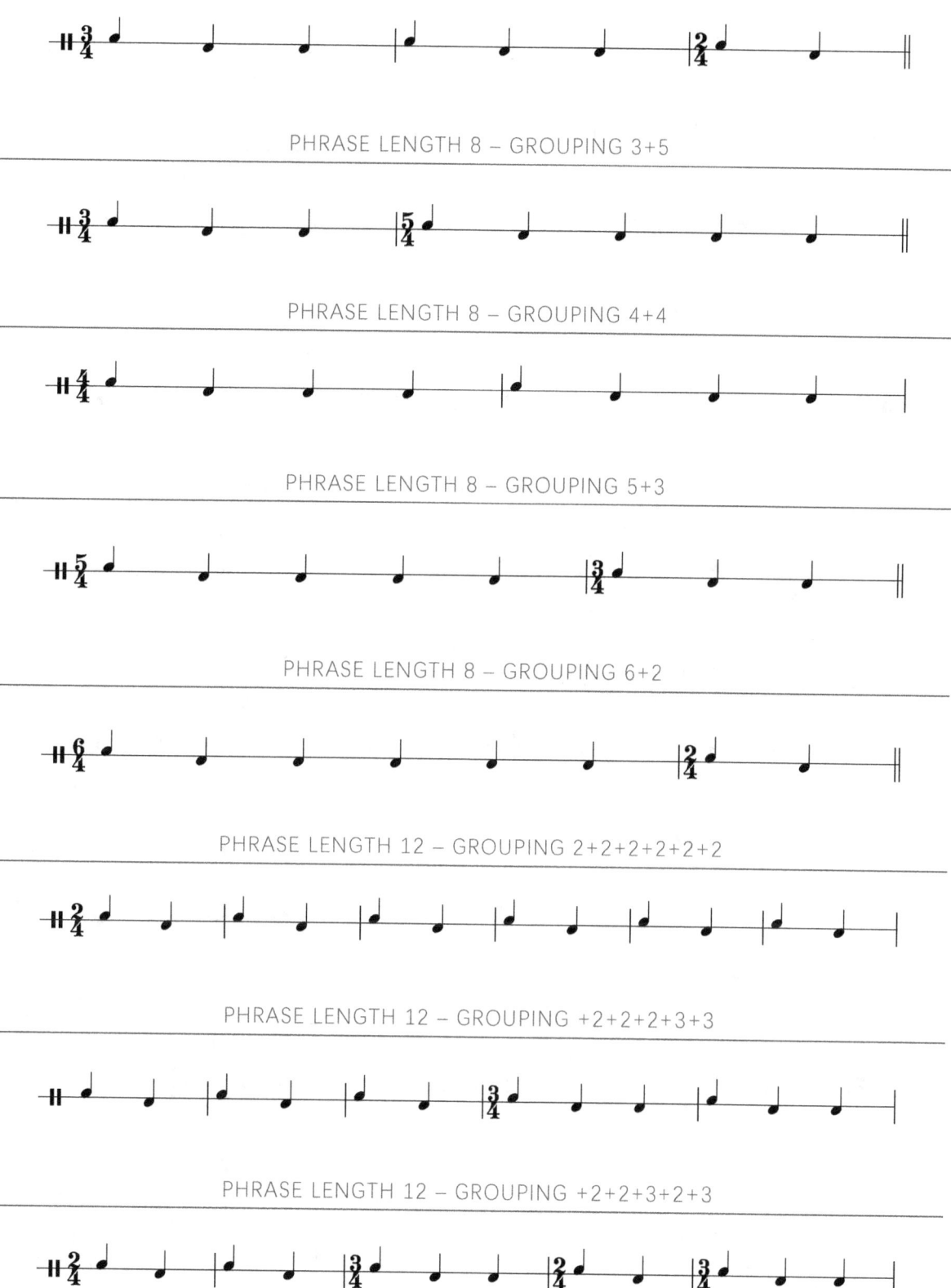

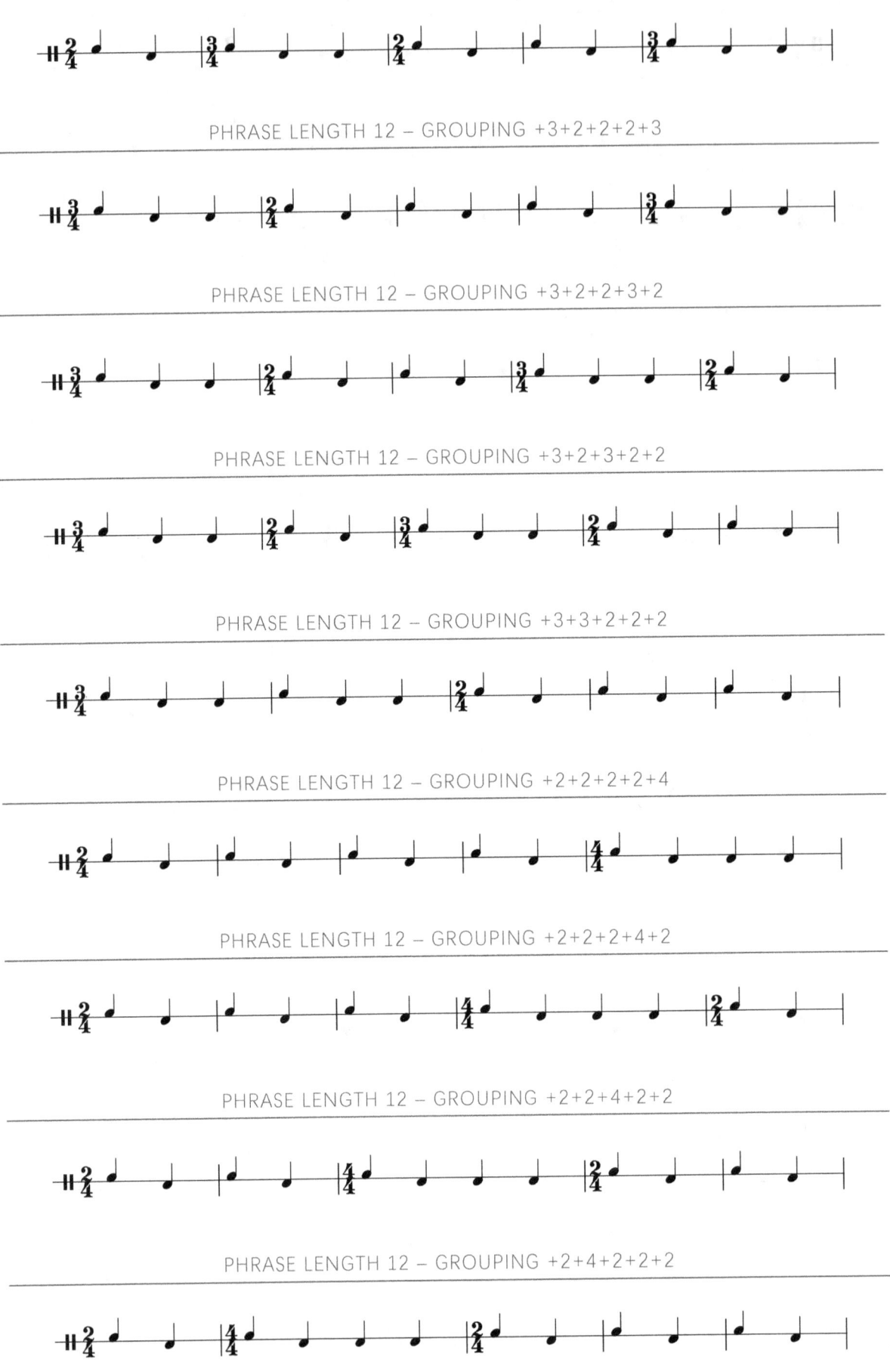

PHRASE LENGTH 12 – GROUPING +4+2+2+2+2

PHRASE LENGTH 12 – GROUPING +2+2+4+4

PHRASE LENGTH 12 – GROUPING +2+4+2+4

PHRASE LENGTH 12 – GROUPING +4+2+2+4

PHRASE LENGTH 12 – GROUPING +4+2+4+2

PHRASE LENGTH 12 – GROUPING +4+4+2+2

PHRASE LENGTH 12 – GROUPING +2+3+3+4

PHRASE LENGTH 12 – GROUPING +2+3+4+3

PHRASE LENGTH 12 – GROUPING +2+4+3+3

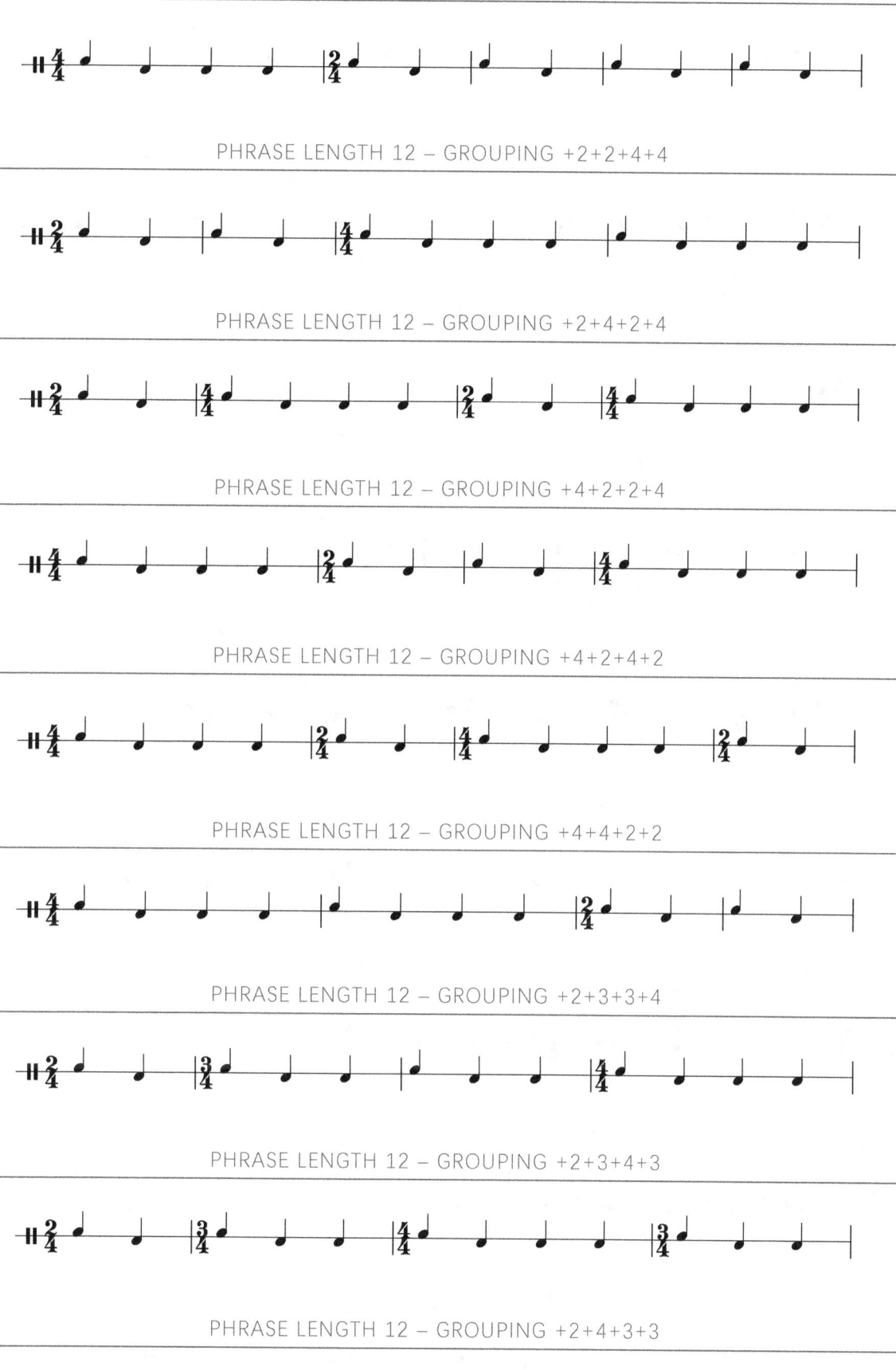

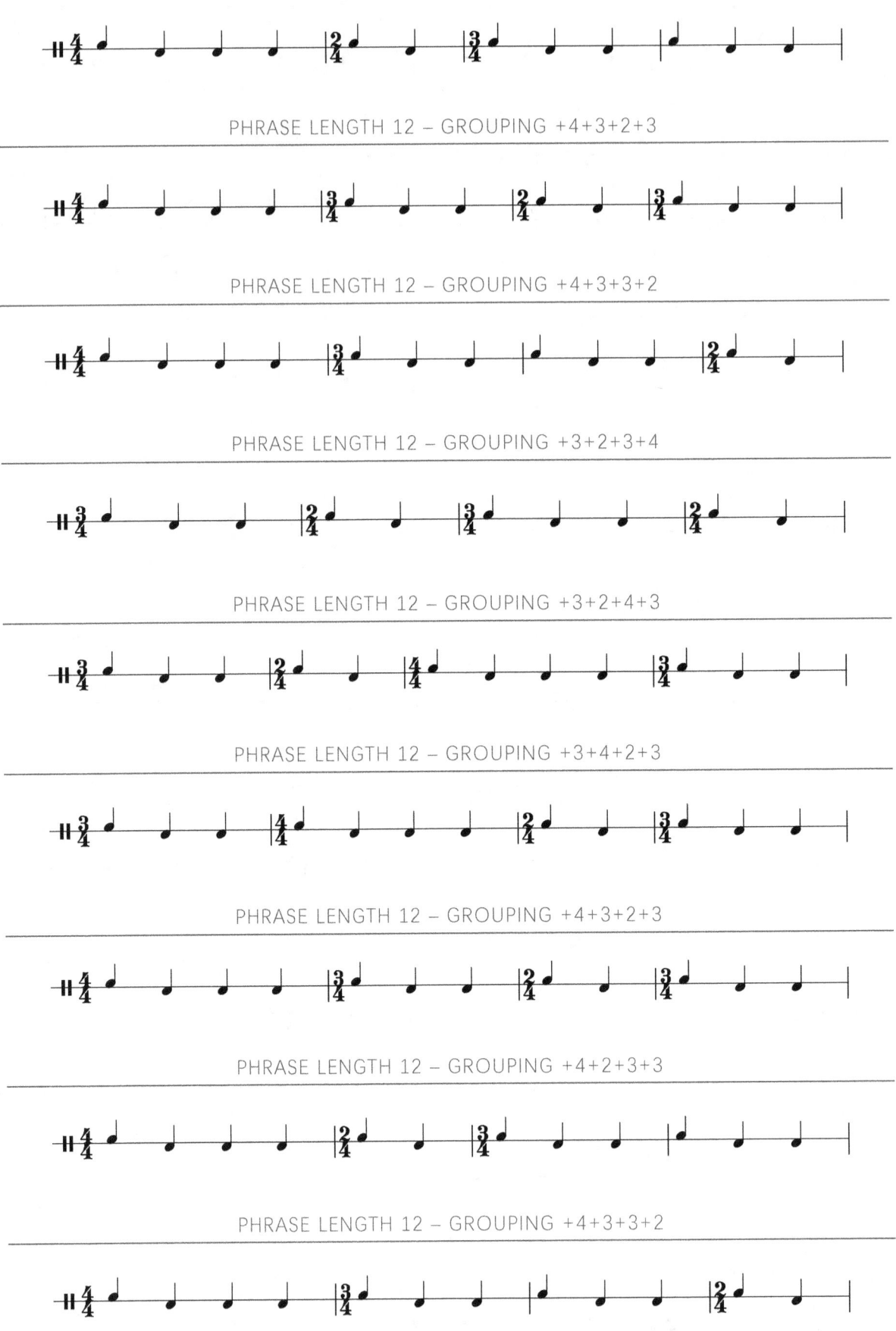

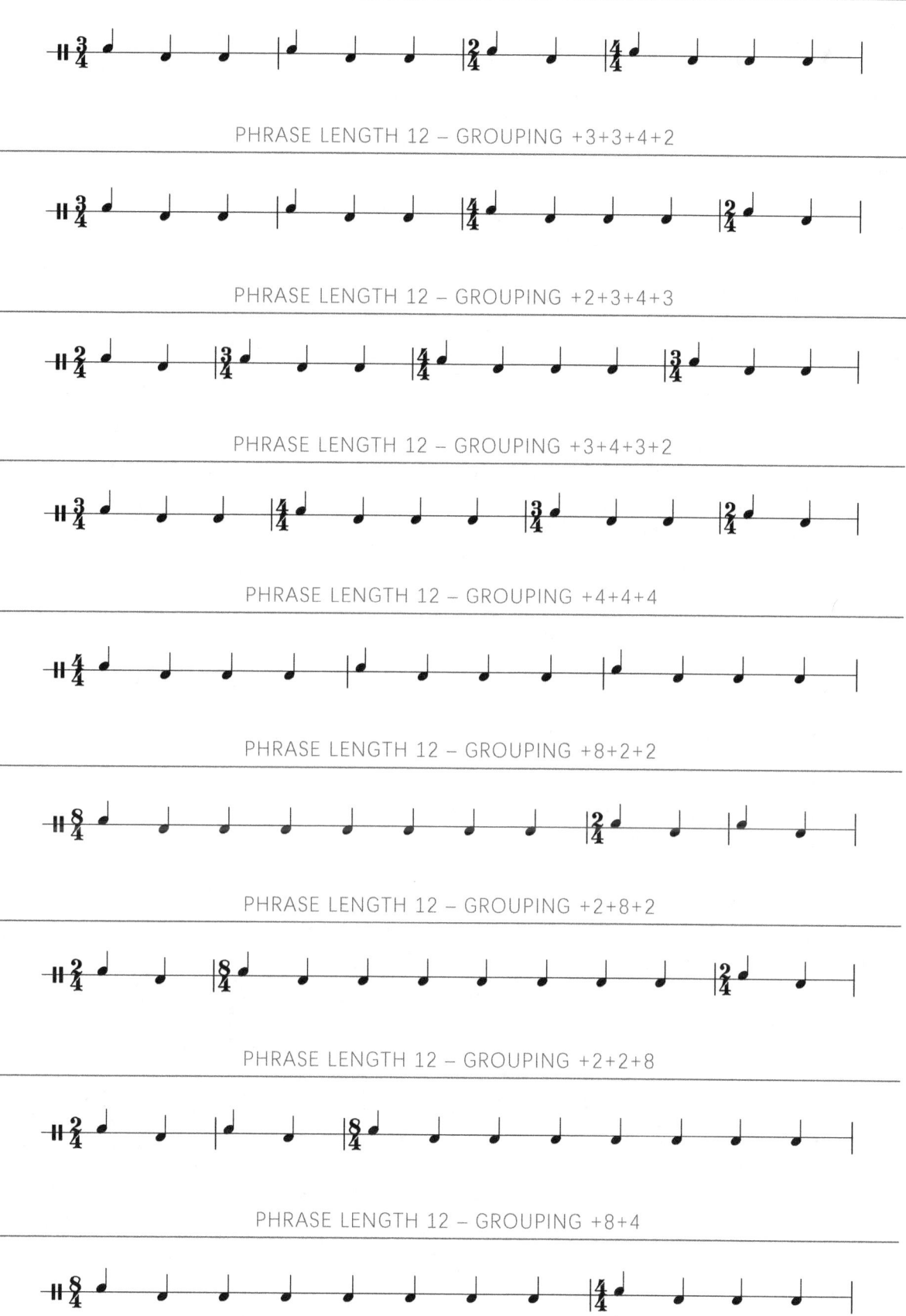

PHRASE LENGTH 12 – GROUPING +4+8

TONE GROUPS

Tone groups exist within the beat groups. They can be used to expand the beats via improvisation. The Tone group is the equivalent of a bar in western music.

This example uses the first beat group of the Bābǎn (八板) mother tune.

Here is the same tune but with the addition of Tone Groups. Tone groups could be created as motifs.

Here is a different set of tone groups for the same Bābǎn (八板) group, this time using different scales and modes. The changes here are shown within a beat group. But the changes can happen between beat groups.

The mode of the tone group is set by the start and end notes of the group.

The process of embellishing the tune is called Adding Characters (Tiānzì, 添字) or Subtracting Characters (Jiǎnzì, 减字).

Examples of Adding Characters are shown below. Some of the sections now have quavers or dotted rhythms. Variation 2 is more embellished than Variation 1.

Examples of Subtracting Characters are shown below. In the first variation the melody lines are mashed together by removing the end minims. In the second the longer melody lines of the first variation are shortened by removing notes.

Adding variations can be used as a purely musical endeavour, but variations can also be used to add groups for Tone Singing.

TONE SINGING (TUŌQIĀNG, 拖腔)

A melisma is a musical phrase that is sung for a single syllable of text. In Chinese Music the words are tonal. Mandarin has four tones; Cantonese has six tones; and dialects closer to old Chinese have eight tones. However, when the music is sung as a simple melody it contains no tonal information. This makes it hard for the listener to identify the meaning of the words. One approach is to use a standard melisma to indicate the tone of the word. While it is used, there is much debate as to how common this practice was. Here we will describe how it is used.

This use of a melisma to indicate the tone is called Tone Singing (Tuōqiāng, 拖腔). For music with words, it is not unusual for a tone group to be the same as a melisma.

There seems to be a reasonable principle at work here, which can be described as: use the rules for tone singing unless the rules result in a displeasing melody. Make whatever changes are necessary to produce a pleasing melody and ignore the Tone Singing rules for that part of the melody.

Mandarin has four tones. The tones are: (1) a flat high tone; (2) a tone rising in pitch from low to high; (3) a tone that dips from mid to low before going to high; and (4) a tone the goes from high to low. As a rudimentary example, we might represent the tone melismas as the following note sequences. Typically, the sequences are richer and more complex.

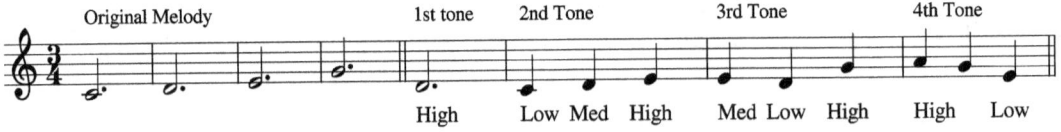

In this Mandarin dialect example: (1) First tone, which is high, is a tone above the required note; (2) Second tone which is low to high is a sequence of note from one tone below to one tone above; (3) Third tone which is med-low-high is the actual note, a note below and then a note above; and (4) fourth tone which is high to low is the sequence one tone above, the actual tone and then one tone below.

Cantonese has six tones with five pitch levels. The five pitch levels are: (1) High, (2) mid/high, (3) mid, (4) mid/low, and (5) low. A simplistic melisma could look like.

In this Cantonese tone example: (1) First tone is high; (2) Second tone is mid to high/mid to high; (3) Third tone is mid; (4) Fourth tone it mid/low to low; (5) Fifth tone is mid/low to mid; and (6) Sixth tone is mid/low.

As English words use tone to express emotional content, an extension of this is to have the melisma indicate the emotion of the word.

For a melisma the following terms can be used: the first note is called Tone Singing Start (Qiāngtóu 腔头); the last note is called Tone Singing End (Qiāngwěi 腔尾). If the word starts on the first beat of a phrase it is called Correct Frame (Zhèngbǎn 正版).

TONE GROUP EXPANSIONS

A melisma for the tone singing can be fitted into the tune. But this is not always possible when fitting new words to an old tune. In such a case, the tune can be expanded by inserting notes. Conversely, if there are fewer words than the tune has notes, the tune can be shortened by removing notes.

Within the Chinese Musical Canon there are several approaches to implement this insertion and removal of notes. Note that adding a note to say a 4/4 bar would make the bar 5/4.

Some of the principles used in the section Beat and Time (page 54) can be used here. There are also the following traditional methods.

In addition to whole note intervals, glides are common when singing to give the notes tonal information.

Expand the first beat to one and a half beats or two beats making the first beat of a tone group longer. This is called Leading Beat Side (Cètóuyǎn, 侧头眼).

Expand the last beat to one and a half or two beats. This is called Final Beat Side (侧末眼, Cèmòyǎn).

Singing two consecutive sixteenth notes in the first half of the last beat of the melisma is called Pinch Tune (Cuōqiāng, 撮腔). This could be combined with the half note version of Final Beat Side (Cèmòyǎn, 侧末眼) to add the additional eighth note for the two sixteenth notes.

Adding a leading note between a minor third and perfect fourth interval is called a Fill Note (Diànqiāng, 垫腔). The only two modes with a minor third and a perfect fourth are Jiǎo Mode (角调) and Yǔ Mode (羽调).

Adding a passing note between a gap of a minor third is called a Fill Gap Note (垫音, diànyīn). In any five-tone scale there are two such minor third gaps. They are the intervals Jiǎo (角) to Zhǐ (徵), and Yǔ (羽) to Gōng (宫). There are two semitones in these intervals. The scale being used will determine which note is the correct note to use. The passing notes are: (1) the fourth note (Biànzhǐ, 变徵); (2) the sharp fourth note (Biànzhēng, 变征); (3) the flat seventh note (Rùn, 闰); and (4) the seventh note (Biàngōng, 变宫).

RHYTHMIC GROUPS

The pattern of music can be enhanced by adding and removing beats from the bars or Tone Groups[9].

Typically, this approach to Rhythm Groups is applied to drumbeats. in the first half we add one and in the second half we remove one beat for each successive bar. The sequence starts at 1 beat, increments to 4 beats and then decrements back ton 1 beat.

The example I give here is for adding and removing two notes from each bar.

PERCUSSION (LUÓGǓDIǍN, 锣鼓点)

Percussion is used in Chinese music to fulfil more functions than in Western Music. It is used to (1) keep the beat, (2) mark the start or the end of a section of music, (3) to provide background ambience, and (4) to provide situational cues. In this regard it also takes the role that harmony performs in Western Music to provide sonic contrast and a sense of motion.

---

[9] This approach to rhythm is typically used in Chinese standing ensemble who may move around town.

Predefined percussion rhythms are called Fixed Pattern Percussion Rhythms (Luógǔdiǎn, 锣鼓点). Such a percussion group might include drum, clapper, small cymbal, small gong, and large gong.

Situational cues or musical gestures include: (1) ambience, such as a thunderstorm or waves; (2) punctuation of a speech, or dramatic movement; (3) denote a persona; denote a social class; or (4) indicate a state of mind.

The rhythms here are a selection of the ones used. The actual rhythms vary from ensemble to ensemble and across musical styles.

If the drum pattern rhythm is too short, you can extend it by repeating bars within the pattern.

PERCUSSION AS BACKGROUND AMBIENCE

This section includes a new notation. This is a special set of characters used for the percussion section. The section after this one includes the characters used and their meaning.

RIOT OF HAMMERS (LUÀNCHUÍ, 乱锤)

A moment of confusion can be indicated by the Riot of Hammers (Luànchuí, 乱锤). It is played with a gong.

NINE AND A HALF HAMMERS (JIǓCHUÍBÀN, 九锤半)

Nine and a Half Hammers (Jiǔchuíbàn, 九锤半) is used to: (1) match a person's panicked movement in the dark; (2) match the opening of martial arts, water warfare, competition, changing clothes, etc.; or (3) match characters in funny singing.

LIGHT HURRICANE (YĪNLUÓ, 阴锣)

The Light Hurricane drum pattern (Yīnluó, 阴锣) is used to match hidden or slow movements, such as dressing up, searching in the dark, looking for objects, or jumping. The term Yīn (阴) refers to the light hit of the gong and cymbals.

SKEWER (CHUÀNZI, 串子)

This is the Skewer drum pattern (Chuànzi, 串子).

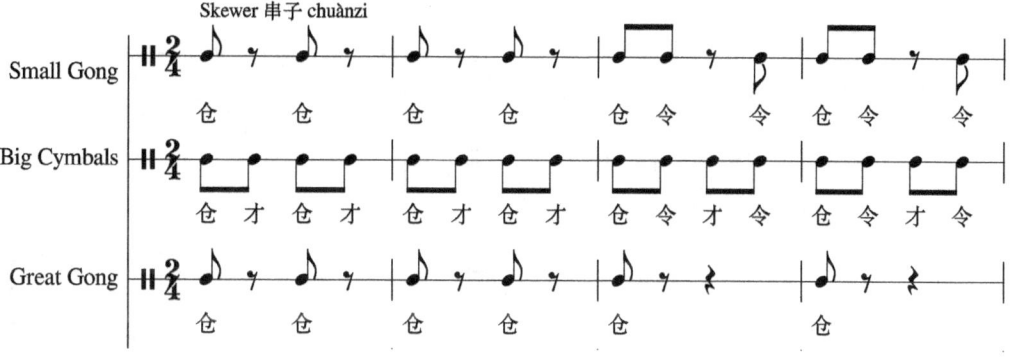

FOUR HEAD STRIKES (SÌJĪTÓU, 四击头)

This is the Four Head Strikes drum pattern (Sìjītóu 四击头)

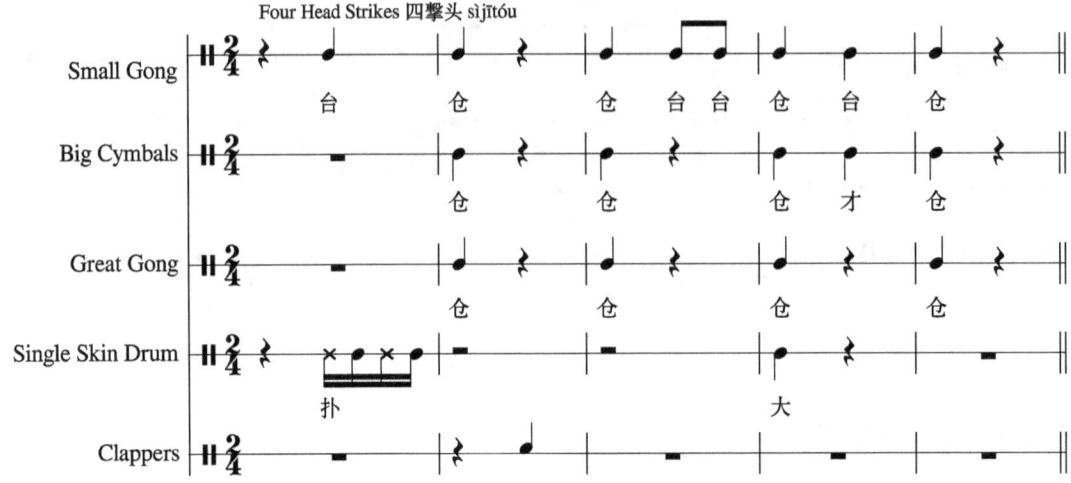

HORSE LEG (MǍTUǏ, 马腿)

Horse Leg drum pattern (Mǎtuǐ, 马腿). This drum pattern is used in aggressive scenes such as combat with sword fights, and physical movements such as jumping and rolling.

PERCUSSION AS PUNCTUATION

Percussion can be used as punctuation. Here are some examples.

Punctuation	Drum Pattern
Comma	台台
Full Stop	大大 | 台台 |

TABLE 21 RHTHMIC PUNCTUATION

Dǐbǎn (底板) is a percussive clapper that is used at the end of a melody to indicate that the melody has ended, particularly when the melody has a free rhythm.

RHYTHMIC CUES

Percussion can be used to give queues about events. It is typically used with live theatrical performance.

The start of a sung word or phrase can be marked by a clapper sound called Sparkle Clapper, Shǎnbǎn (闪板). The end of a sung word or phrase can be indicated by a clapper sound called Stop Clapper, Jiébǎn (截板). Another name for this is Cease Clapper, Juébǎn (绝板).

DRUM NOTATION (LUÓGǓ JĪNG, 锣鼓经)

Luógǔ Jīng (锣鼓经) is the main Chinese Drum notation. Unlike music for other instruments which these days uses Jiǎnpǔ notation. Luógǔ Jīng continues to use the character notation.

This table lists some of the commonly used notes.

Instrument		Part	Note		
板	Bǎn	Clappers	扎	Zhā	Hit loudly
			衣	Yī	Hit lightly
			一	Yī	Hit
板鼓	*Bǎngǔ*	Frame Drum	拉	Lā	Double hit drum roll
			八	Bā	Left hand hit or double hit
			崩	Bēng	Double hit
卜魚 / 板	Bo yú / Bǎn	Fish Board	局	Jú	
			角	Jiǎo	Hit (Cantonese symbol)
			各	Gè	
			大	Dà	Single hit loudly with right mallet
			达	Dá	Intense hit
			答	Dá	Hit
			八	Bā	Double hit with two mallets
			崩	Bēng	
			大八	Dàbā	Loud left and soft right hit
单皮鼓	Dānpí Gǔ	Single Skin Drum	多	Duō	Single hit lightly
			哆	Duō	
			哆罗	Duōluō	Right hand combined hits.
			打	Dǎ	Fast iterations with both mallets (roll)
			嘟	Dū	double stroke roll
			隆咚	Lōngdōng	Heavy then soft hit one after the other with the right hand.
			嘟 儿	Dū Er	Drum roll continuously with two mallets
			空	Kōng	Tap softly.
大锣	Dàluó	Great Gong	冷	Lěng	Hit on the side of the gong.
			扑	Pū	Hit (Mandarin symbol)
大、小 木鱼	Dà, Xiǎo Mùyú	Big and small wooden fish	朴、的	Pǔ, de	Hit (Cantonese symbol)

Instrument Part			Note		
铙钹	Náobó	Big Cymbals	七	Qī	Play solo.
			才	Cái	Single hit
			令	Lìng	Soft hit
			扑	Pū	Single muted hit
沙的雙皮鼓 or 梆鼓	Shāde Shuāngpígǔ or Bānggǔ	Shaker double skin drum / bang drum	的	De	Hit (Cantonese symbol)
			得	Dé	Hit (Cantonese symbol)
檀板	Tánbǎn	Hardwood Clappers	扎	Zhā	Hit loudly
			衣	Yī	Hit lightly
			本	Běn	Hit lightly and continuously
			乙	Yǐ	Hit or a rest
			个	Gè	
小锣	Xiǎoluó	Small Gong	台	Tái	Single hit loudly
			令	Lìng	Tap softly
			匝	Zā	Single muted hit
			另	Lìng	
战鼓	Zhàngǔ	War Drum	东	Dōng	Hit (Cantonese symbol)

TABLE 22 SINGLE INSTRUMENT PERCUSSION NOTES

Ensemble Part			Note		
大锣 / 小锣 / 钹	Dàluó / Xiǎoluó / Bó	Great Gong and Small Gong and Cymbals	仓	Cāng	Play together loudly - The great gong may lead. The small gong and cymbals are optional. Alternatively, a single hit on the big gong.
			匡	Kuāng	Muted hits
			空	Kōng	Muffled hits
			倾	Qīng	Tap - The small gong and cymbals are optional.
大锣 / 铙钹 / 小锣	Dàluó / Náobó	Great Gong, Big Cymbals and small gong.	顷	Qǐng	Tap the great gong and strike the cymbals and small gong.
			空	Kōng	Hit the great gong and strike the cymbals and small gong.
小锣 / 钹	Xiǎoluó / Bó	Small Gong and Cymbals	才	Cái	Play together or just cymbal.
			七	Qī	

TABLE 23 ENSEMBLE PERCUSSION NOTES

MELODIES AND CHORDS

Within the limitation of the Positive Notes of the Pentatonic Scale a limited set of chords are available. Various chords only exist in particular modes. To use a particular chord, use the correct mode. This chart shows the full set of chords available and the modes that support those chords.

		Chord[10]		Mode	Jiǎnpǔ Notes	Nashville Number
			宮	Gōng	1-3-5	1
宮	Gōng	major	角	Jiǎo	3-5-1	3
			徵	Zhǐ	5-1-3	5
宮	Gōng	major add 6	宮	Gōng	1-3-5-6	1^6
			角	Jiǎo	3-5-6-1	3^6
			宮	Gōng	1-2-3-5-6	$1^{6/9}$
宮	Gōng	major add 6/9	商	Shāng	2-3-5-6-1	$2^{6/9}$
			角	Jiǎo	3-5-6-1-2	$3^{6/9}$
			宮	Gōng	1-2-3	1^9
			宮	Gōng	1-2-3-5	1^9
			商	Shāng	2-3-1	2^9
宮	Gōng	major add 9	商	Shāng	2-3-5-1	2^9
			角	Jiǎo	3-1-2	3^9
			角	Jiǎo	3-5-1-2	3^9
			徵	Zhǐ	5-1-2-3	5^9
宮	Gōng	sus2	宮	Gōng	1-2-5	1^{sus2}
			商	Shāng	2-5-1	2^{sus2}
宮	Gōng	add6 sus2	宮	Gōng	1-2-5-6	1^{6sus2}
			宮	Gōng	1-2-6	1^7
商	Shāng	add5/7	商	Shāng	2-6-1	2^7
			羽	Yǔ	6-1-2	6^7
商	Shāng	sus2	商	Shāng	2-3-6	2^{sus2}
			角	Jiǎo	3-6-2	3^{sus2}
商	Shāng	sus4	商	Shāng	2-5-6	2^{sus4}
商	Shāng	add7 sus4	商	Shāng	2-5-6-1	2^7
商	Shāng	add9 sus4	商	Shāng	2-3-5-6	2^{9sus4}
			角	Jiǎo	3-5-6-2	3^{9sus4}
			商	Shāng	2-3-5	$2m^7$
角	Jiǎo	minor7	角	Jiǎo	3-5-2	$3m^7$
			徵	Zhǐ	5-2-3	$5m^7$
徵	Zhǐ	sus2	徵	Zhǐ	5-6-2	5^{sus2}
			羽	Yǔ	6-2-5	6^{sus2}
徵	Zhǐ	add6 sus2	徵	Zhǐ	5-6-2-3	5^{6sus2}
徵	Zhǐ	sus4	徵	Zhǐ	5-1-2	5^{sus4}
徵	Zhǐ	add9 sus4	徵	Zhǐ	5-6-1-2	5^{9sus4}
			羽	Yǔ	6-1-2-5	6^{9sus4}
			宮	Gōng	1-3-6	1m
羽	Yǔ	minor	角	Jiǎo	3-6-1	3m
			羽	Yǔ	6-1-3	6m
羽	Yǔ	minor7	宮	Gōng	1-5-6	$1m^7$

---

[10] Note: where there is no major or minor listed, the chord is ambiguous and could be either. This is because the third is missing.

Chord[10]			Mode		Jiǎnpǔ Notes	Nashville Number
			徵	Zhǐ	5-6-1	$5m^7$
			徵	Zhǐ	5-6-1-3	$5m^7$
			羽	Yǔ	6-1-5	$6m^7$
			羽	Yǔ	6-1-3-5	$6m^7$
羽	Yǔ	minor add7/11	徵	Zhǐ	5-6-1-2-3	$5m^{7/11}$
			羽	Yǔ	6-1-2-3-5	$6m^{7/11}$
			宮	Gōng	1-2-3-6	$1m^{11}$
羽	Yǔ	minor add11	商	Shāng	2-3-6-1	$2m^{11}$
			角	Jiǎo	3-6-1-2	$3m^{11}$
			羽	Yǔ	6-1-2-3	$6m^{11}$
羽	Yǔ	sus4	羽	Yǔ	6-2-3	6^{sus4}
			角	Jiǎo	3-5-6	4^7
羽	Yǔ	add5/7	徵	Zhǐ	5-6-3	5^7
			羽	Yǔ	6-3-5	6^{7sus4}
羽	Yǔ	add7 sus4	羽	Yǔ	6-2-3-5	6^{7sus4}

TABLE 24 POSITIVE PENTATONIC CHORDS

The following sections show these chords implemented in the various keys.

C KEY CHORDS (HUÁNG ZHŌNG, 黄钟)

C# KEY CHORDS (DÀ LǙ, 大呂)

D KEY CHORDS (TÀI CÙ, 太簇)

D# KEY CHORDS (JIÁ ZHŌNG, 夹钟)

E KEY CHORDS (GŪ XIĂN, 姑洗)

F KEY CHORDS (ZHÒNG LǙ, 中吕)

F# KEY CHORDS (RUÍ BĪN, 蕤宾)

G KEY CHORDS (LÍN ZHŌNG, 林钟)

G# KEY CHORDS (YÍ ZÉ, 夷则)

A KEY CHORDS (NÁN LǕ, 南吕)

A# KEY CHORDS (WÚ YÌ, 无射)

B KEY CHORDS (YÌNG ZHŌNG, 应钟)

SHORT NOTE INSTRUMENT ARPEGGIOS

Trills and arpeggios are the staple of the short note instruments. The examples here are shown in C Major (Huáng Zhōng, 黄钟) Key. They can be translated to any key.

The 1, 2, 3, 5 and 6 relate to the root note

The line underneath in the 1st mode is the repeating section. Some arpeggios do not repeat from the first note.

REPEATS (ONE NOTE ARPEGGIOS)

On some instruments that do not have good sustain, a long note can be played as a single note constantly and quickly repeated.

An approach is to say that, if a note is longer than a beat, then play the note as a repeated note.

TRILLS (TWO NOTE ARPEGGIOS)

In Chinese Music it is quite common to have widely spaced trills.

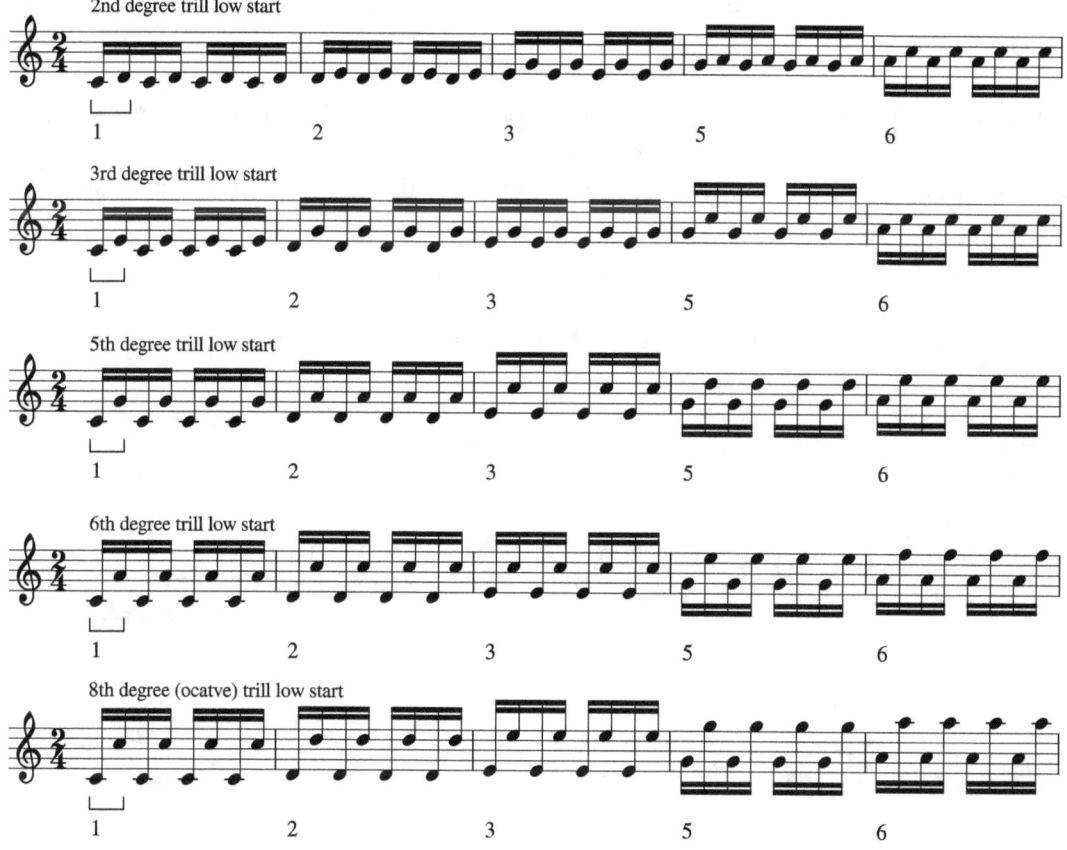

THREE NOTE ARPEGGIOS

The full set of pentatonic arpeggios within a single key are as follows.

			Root		
Sequence	1 Gōng (宫)	2 Shāng (商)	3 Jiǎo (角)	5 Zhǐ (徵)	6 Yǔ (羽)
1-2-3	1-2-3	2-3-5	3-5-6	5-6-1	6-1-2
1-2-5	1-2-5	2-3-6	3-5-1	5-6-2	6-1-3
1-2-6	1-2-6	2-3-1	3-5-2	5-6-3	6-1-5
1-3-5	1-3-5	2-5-6	3-6-1	5-1-2	6-2-3
1-3-6	1-3-6	2-5-1	3-6-2	5-1-3	6-2-5
1-5-6	1-5-6	2-6-1	3-1-2	5-2-3	6-3-5

TABLE 25 THREE NOTE ARPEGGIOS

Within the arpeggios are the following versions.

Sequence	Description
Up arp	The notes are repeatedly played in the ascending sequence.
Up-down arp	The notes are repeatedly played ascending and then descending with no repeated notes.
Down-up arp	The notes are repeatedly played descending and then ascending with no repeated notes.
Down arp	The notes are repeatedly played in the descending sequence.
Up arp / trill low start	The lowest note is played and then the top two notes are repeatedly played, starting on the lower note.
Up arp / trill high start	The lowest note is played and then the top two notes are repeatedly played, starting on the higher note.
Down arp / trill low start	The highest note is played and then the lower two notes are repeatedly played, starting on the lower note.
Down arp / trill high start	The highest note is played and then the lower two notes are repeatedly played, starting on the higher note.

TABLE 26 ARPEGGIO SEQUENCES

The examples here are given for the modes of C Major (Huáng Zhōng, 黄钟) key.

1-2-3 ARPEGGIO

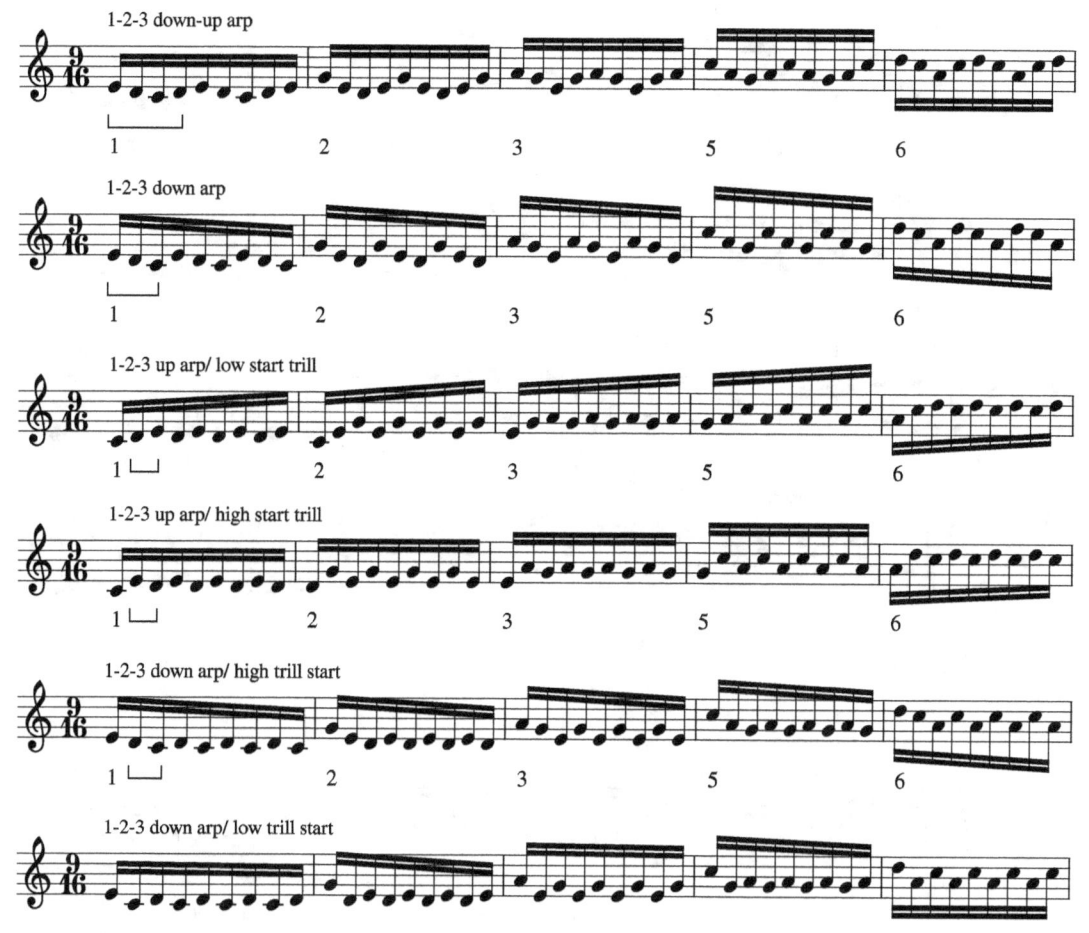

1-2-5 ARPEGGIO

1-2-6 ARPEGGIO

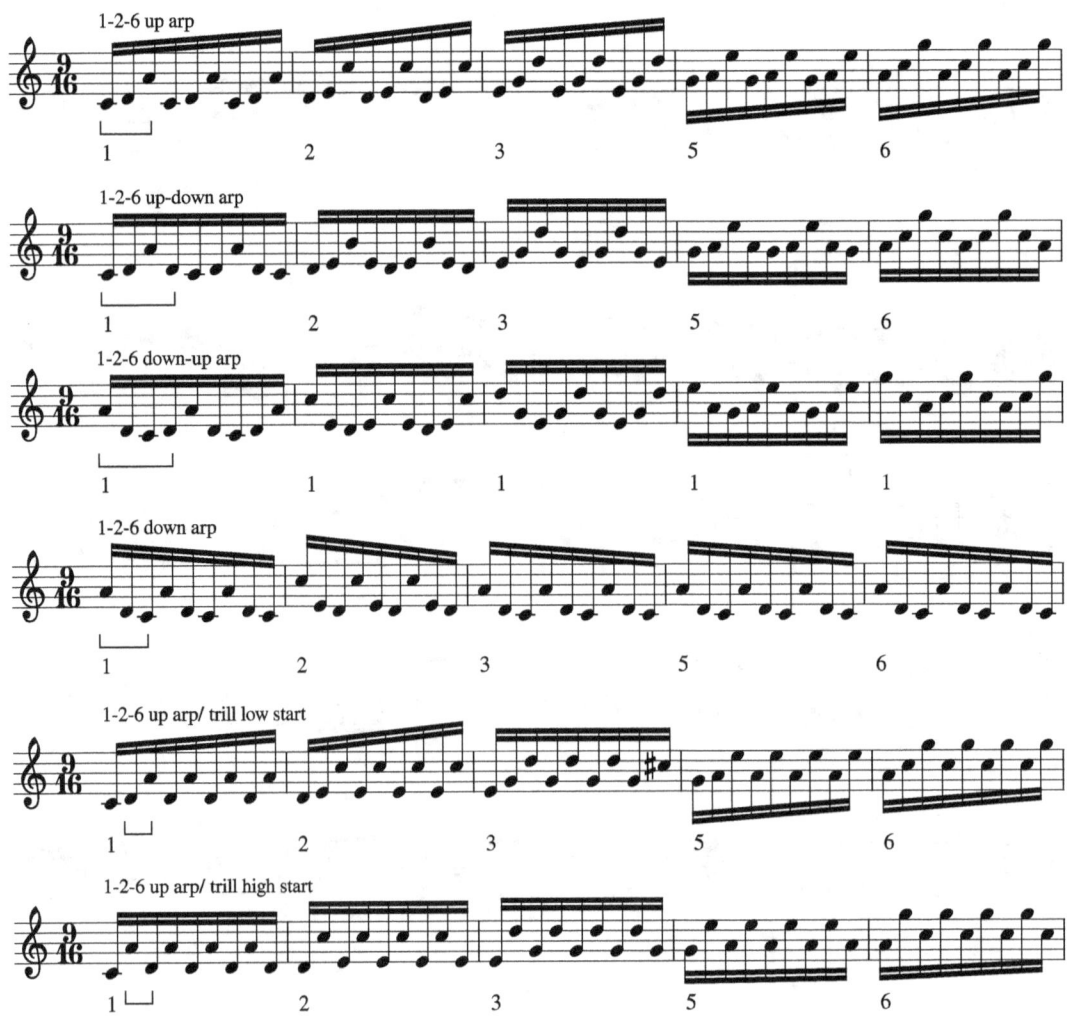

1-2-6 down arp/ trill low start

1-2-6 down arp/ trill high start

1-3-5 ARPEGGIO

1-3-5 up arp

1-3-5 up-down arp

1-3-5 down-up arp

1-3-5 down arp

1-3-5 up arp/ trill low start

1-3-5 up arp/ trill high start

1-3-5 down arp/ trill low start

1-3-5 down arp/ trill high start

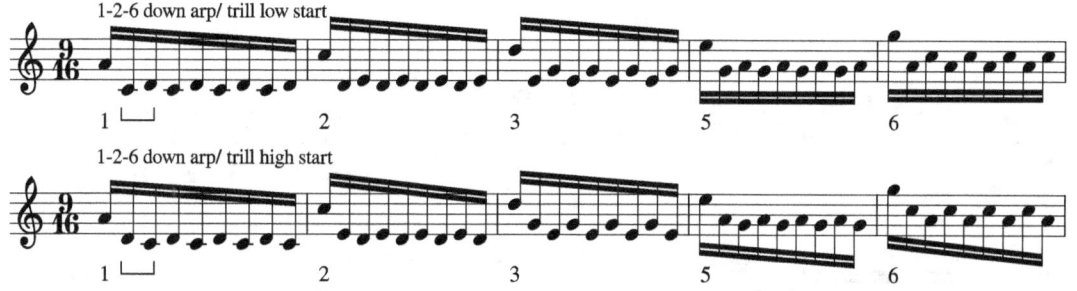

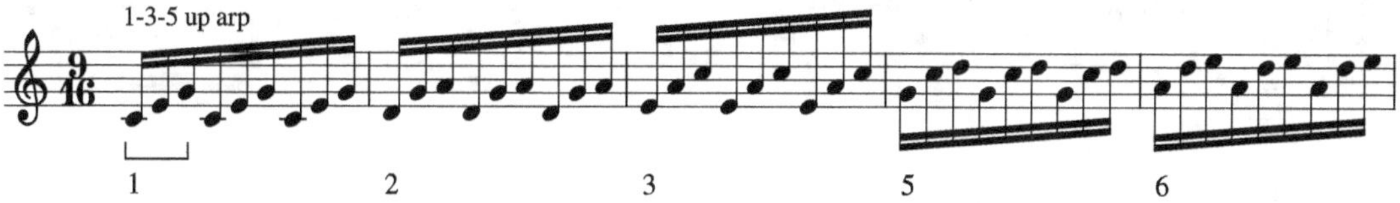

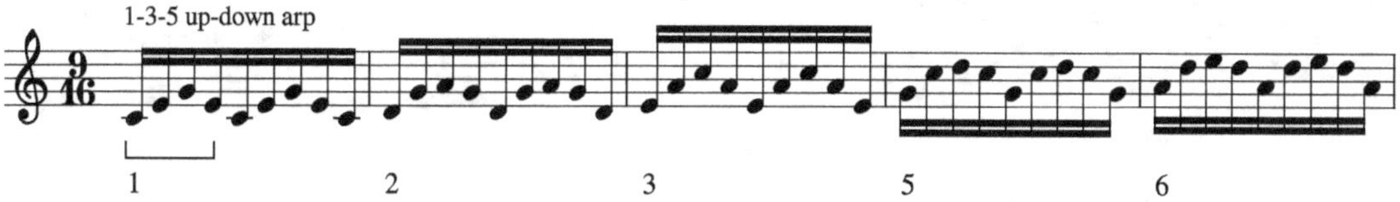

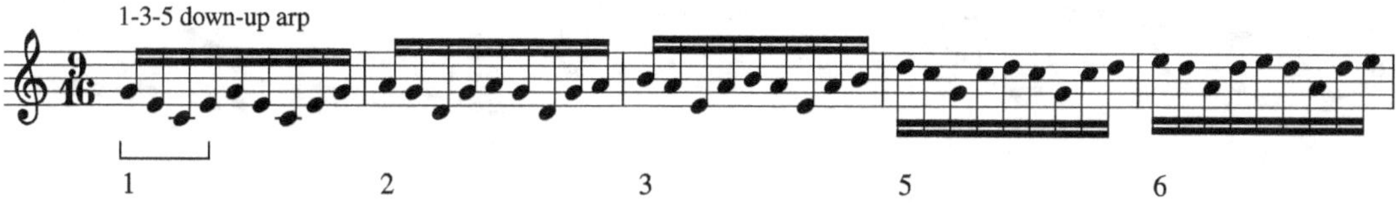

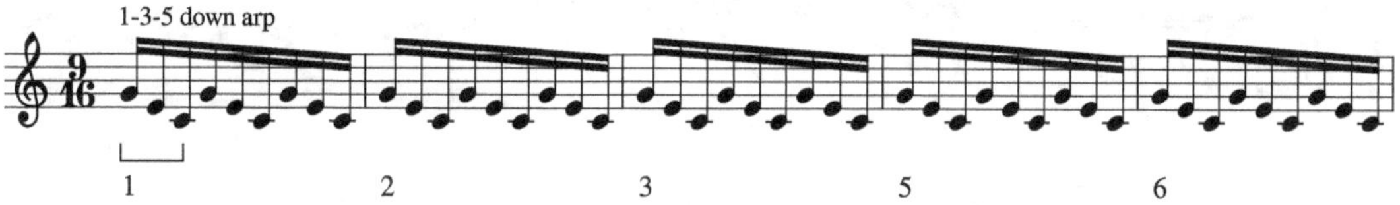

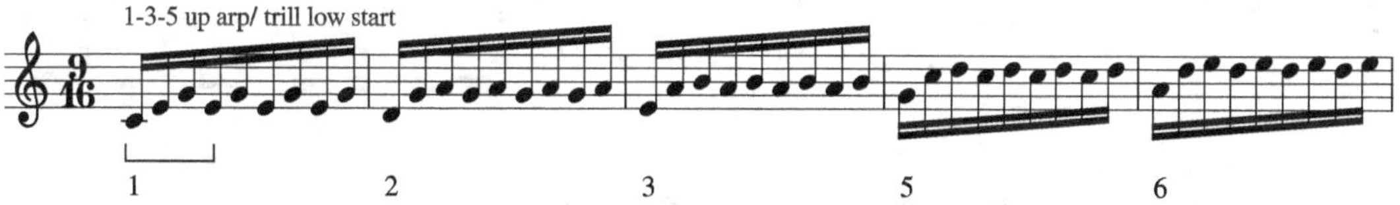

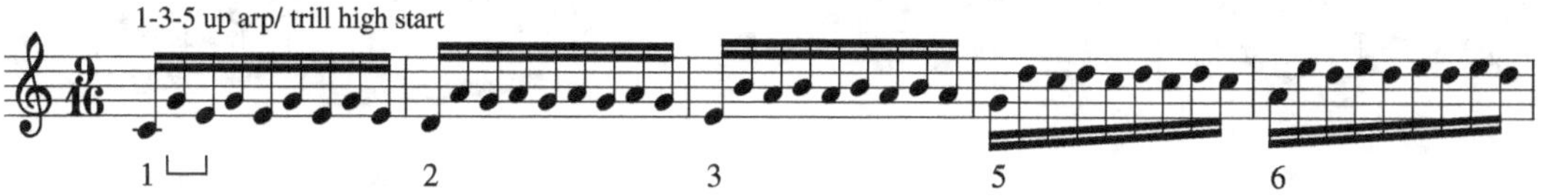

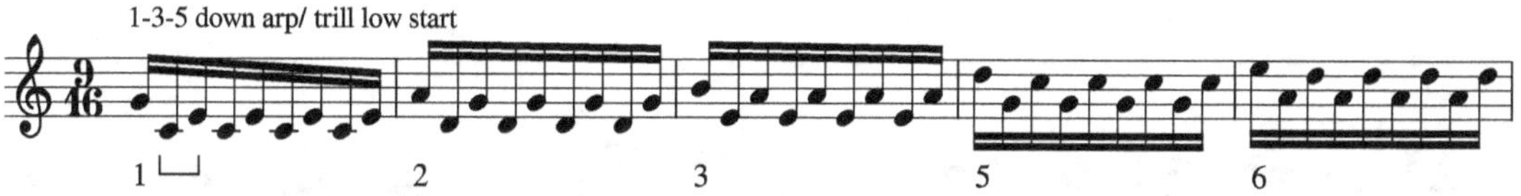

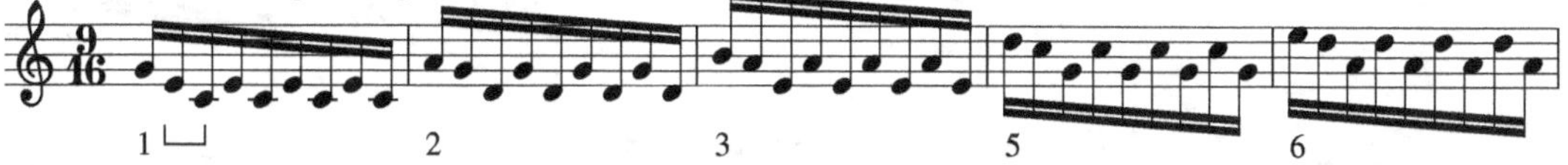

1-3-6 ARPEGGIO

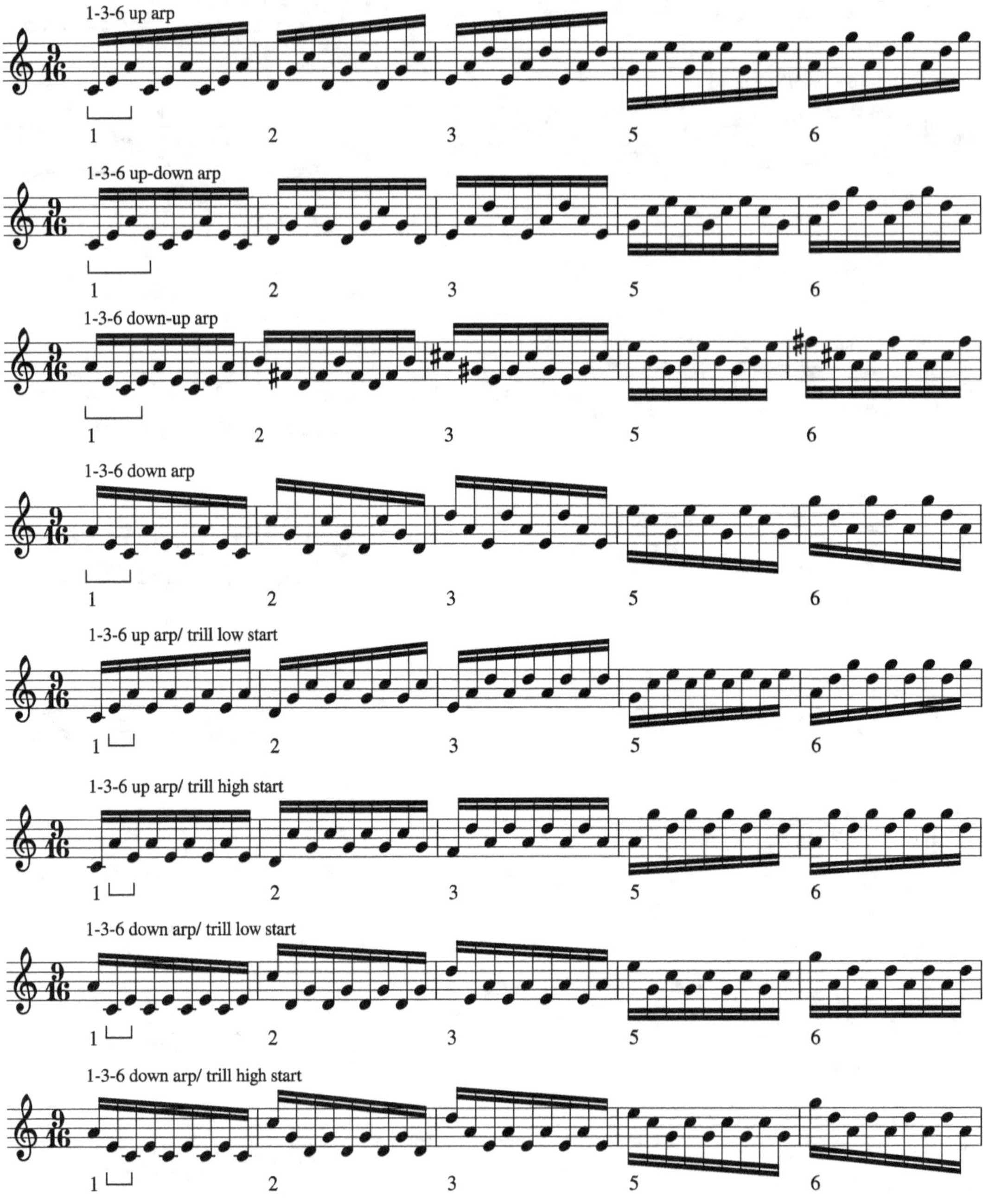

1-5-6 ARPEGGIO

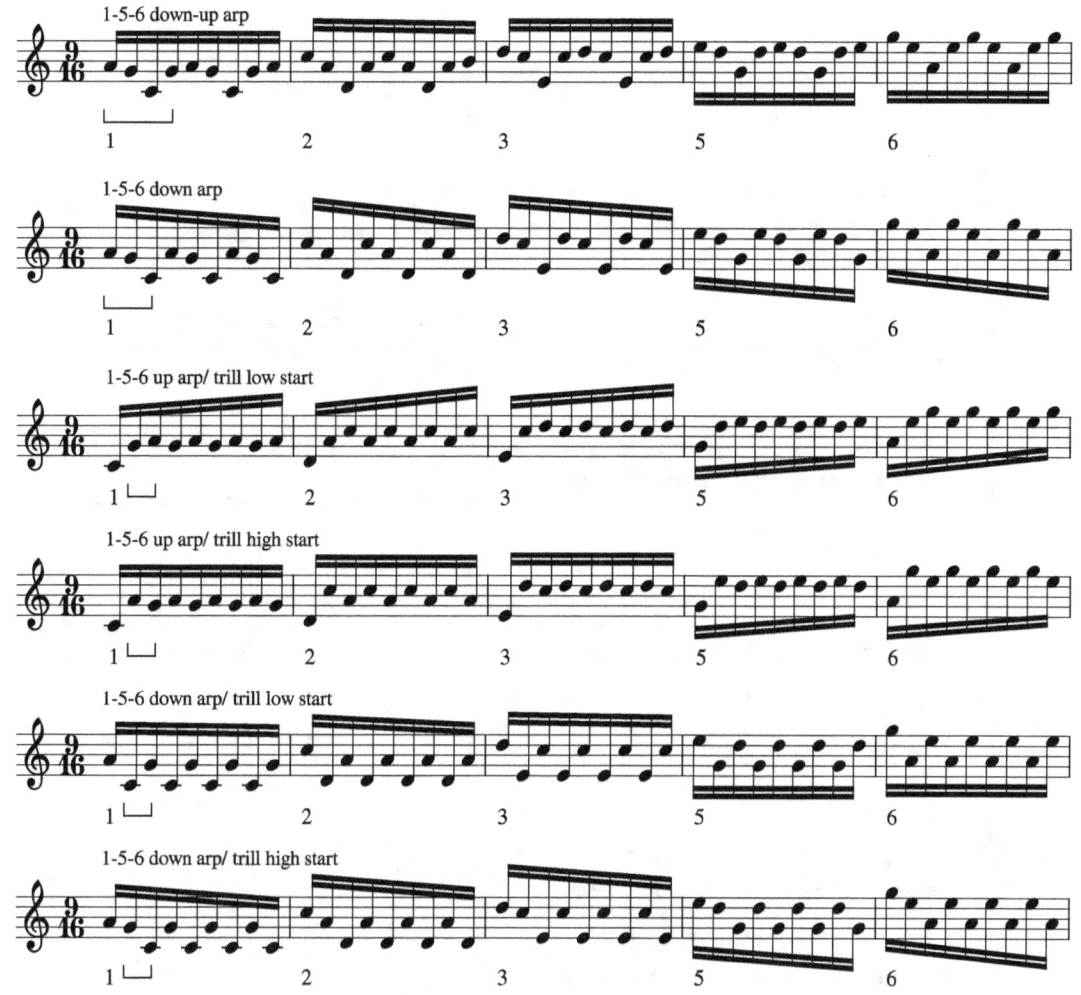

SHORT NOTE INSTRUMENT CHORDS

Short note instruments play chords by rapid repetition of notes. This is based on a hammered dulcimer style instrument that can only play two simultaneous notes per instrument.

The examples here are given for the chords of the C Major (Huáng Zhōng, 黄钟) key.

THREE NOTE CHORDS

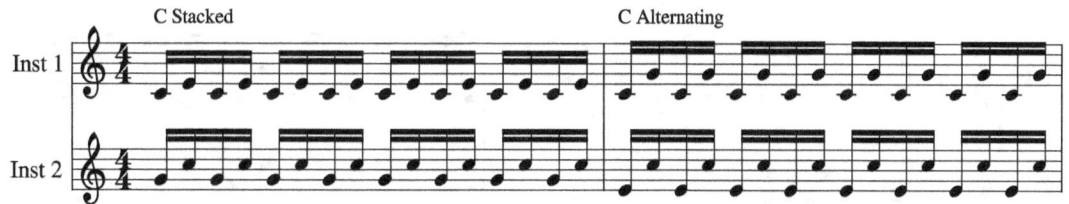

FOUR NOTE CHORDS

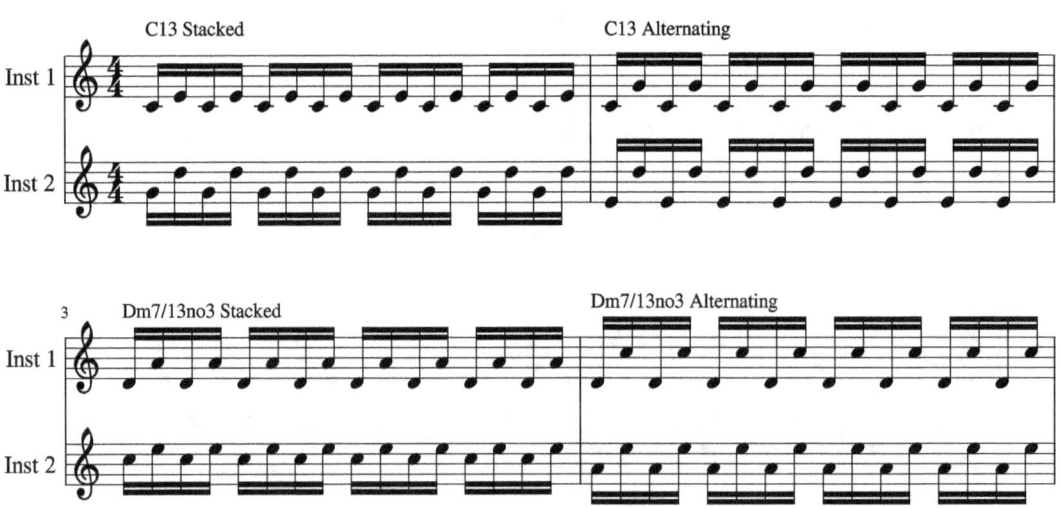

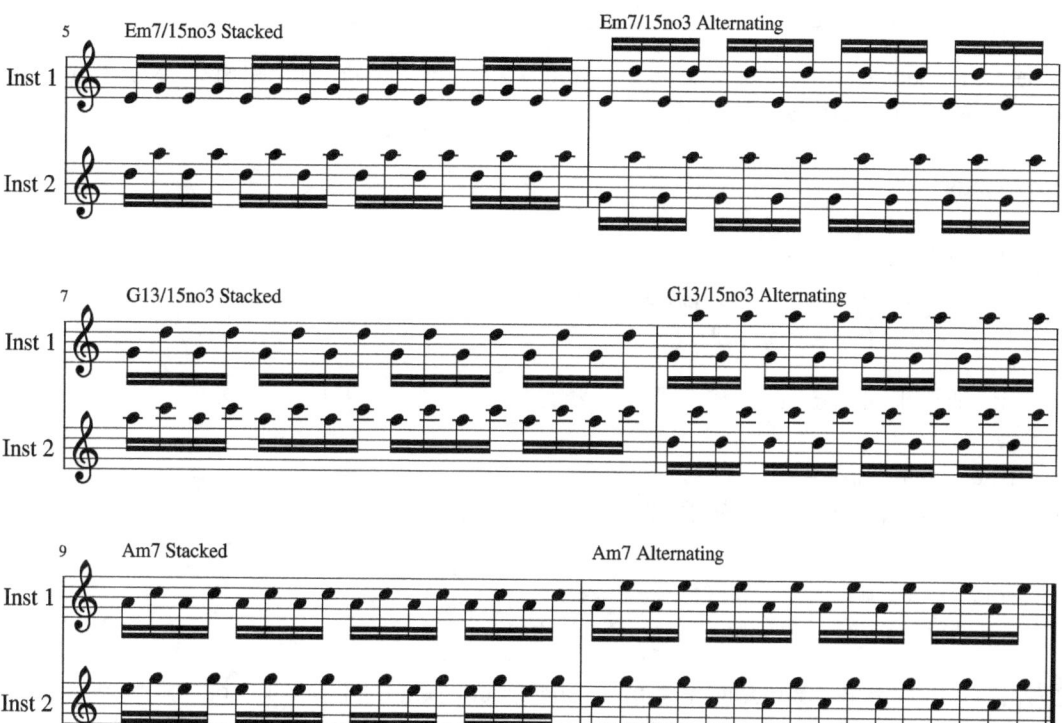

MELODIES (QǓPÁI, 曲牌) AND SUITES (ZǓQǓ, 组曲)

Qǔpái (曲牌) are labelled melodies. They are standard tunes that can be embellished by performers and joined together to form suites.

Types of Songs:

- Working songs (Hàozi, 號子);
- Mountain songs (Shāngē, 山歌), also known as folk songs, and
- Small ditties (Xiǎodiào, 小調).

An alternate classification system is:

- Traditional instrumental pieces;
- Traditional melodies (Qǔpái, 曲牌) pieces;
- Buddhist pieces;
- Folk songs (Shāngē, 山歌) and dances, and
- Instrumental opera imitation pieces (Kǎxì, 咔戏).

Dǎpǔ (打谱) is the process of modifying a traditional Qǔpái to fit the lyrics or needs of the new piece of music. All the information about how to add and remove notes and whole sections from the Qǔpái are specifically for this purpose. Typically, this is done when a new lyric is fitted to an old tune.

Jíqū (集曲) is a Qǔpái that is modified by adding lines from a different Qǔpái.

SUITE FORMS (ZǓQǓ, 组曲)

A suite is made up of several Qǔpái (曲牌).

Form
联曲体	Liánqūtǐ	Linked melody form. For example: A+B+C+D
子母调	Zǐmǔdiào	Alternating melody form. For example: A+B+A1+C+B1
变奏曲	Biànzòuqǔ	Variations on a single theme. For example: A+A1+A2+A

A bìqū (毕曲) is the last tune in a Qǔpái suite.

A sànxù (散序) is an unmetered prelude to a suite.

Yǐnzi (引子) is the introduction to a Qǔpái.

EIGHT BEATS (BĀBǍN, 八板,)

Bābǎn (八板) is a folk song typically used as a dance piece in Beijing Opera.

Alternative names include: Pèng bābǎn (碰八板), Lǎo liù bǎn (老六板), and Lǎo bābǎn (老八板).

Bābǎn structure for 68 beats.

八板 Bābǎn Eight Beats

Phrase	Beats	Beat Grouping
1	8	3+2+3
2	8	3+2+3
3	8	4+4
4	8	3+2+3
5	12	3+2+3+4
6	8	4+4
7	8	5+3
8	8	4+4

A THOUSAND BUDDHAS (QIAN SHENG FÚ, 千声佛)

JASMINE FLOWER PIANO ARRANGEMENT (MÒLÌHUA, 茉莉花)

This piano arrangement uses theory from this book to add a piano arrangement to the original melody that is shown in the vocal line.

INVERSE SCALE MODES

An inversion is created by going down rather than up by the same semitone interval.

Mode		Scale Mode	Inverse Scale Mode	Inverse Mode	
宫	Gōng	Ionian	Phrygian	角	Jiǎo
商	Shāng	Dorian	Dorian	商	Shāng
角	Jiǎo	Phrygian	Ionian	宫	Gōng
变徵	*Biànzhǐ*	*Lydian*	*Locrian*	变宫	*Biàngōng*
徵	Zhǐ	Mixolydian	Aeolian	羽	Yǔ
羽	Yǔ	Aeolian	Mixolydian	徵	Zhǐ
变宫	*Biàngōng*	*Locrian*	*Lydian*	变徵	*Biànzhǐ*

TABLE 27 SCALE INVERSIONS

HISTORICAL BACKGROUND

I did not intend to include a lot of history in this book. But the system is a mishmash of its past influences and I think understanding how this came to be is very informative in reading the technical notes.

The basic Chinese music system uses the pentatonic scale within a twelve-tone system. This pentatonic scale uses notes tuned using Pythagorean[11] tuning, though over the centuries there have been many other tuning methods employed.

The music was written down by the Zhou dynasty (7th to 3rd century BC). The old twelve-tone system is called Lǜlǚ (律吕). It refers to the twelve bamboo pitch pipes. The odd numbered pipes are lǜ (律) and the even numbered pipes are lǚ (吕). What is called the five-tone system in this book, evolved from the Step Names (Jiēmíng, 阶名).

Instruments tuned to a twelve-tone system, such as the pipa, were introduced into China as far back as the Han Dynasty (2nd century AD). The origin of these instruments is uncertain.

A heptatonic notation system was introduced from the Buddhist Kuchan kingdom in Central Asia. The Kuchan kingdom was absorbed into China during the Tang Dynasty (7th century AD) and the notation is is called Kucha notation (Qiūcí, 龜兹). This notation is based on the Indian twelve-tone system.

The Mongolians introduced another heptatonic notation when they conquered China to form the Ming Dynasty (14th to 17th centuries AD).

NOTATION SYSTEMS

This book is written using modern Western Music Notation. In Chinese Music there are several notation systems used. The table here shows the more common ones.

The main notation system used these days in China is called Jiǎnpǔ (简谱) notation. It uses the numbers 1 through 7 to describe the notes C through to B. A dot is placed above and below the number to indicate

---

[11] Note that the Chinese tuning was created independently of Pythagoras. I just use the name Pythagoras as it is the name given to this tuning in the Western System.

an octave higher or an octave lower. The software I am using cannot place a dot directly above or directly below a number. Instead the notation is: `1'` means one octave above, `1̣` means one octave below.

The standard Gōngchě (工尺) notation is based on a Mongolian Notation system that was introduced when Mongolia conquered China and created the Ming Dynasty.

In Gōngchě Pǔ (工尺譜) there is a note, a sharp fa (#4) called gōu (勾). This was introduced by the Ming from the Mongolian script and subsequently fell out of use.

12 TET	Standard Gōngchě	Cantonese Opera Gōngchě	Jiǎnpǔ	Step Names	Five Tone	Solfège
C2	上	伬	1̣		下宫	do
D2	尺	仕	2̣		下商	re
E2	工	亿	3̣		下角	mi
F2	凡	仕	4̣		下变徵	fa
G2	合	伏	5̣		下徵	sol
A3	四	仜	6̣		下羽	la
B3	一	伝	7̣		下变宫	ti
C3	上	合	1	宫	宫	do
D3	尺	士	2	商	商	re
E3	工	乙	3	角	角	mi
F3	凡	上	4	和	变徵	fa
F#3	勾			中		
G3	六	尺	5	徵	徵	sol
A4	五	工	6	羽	羽	la
A#4				闰		
B4	乙	反	7	变	变宫	ti
C4	仕	六	1'		清宫	do
D4	伬	五	2'		清商	re
E4	仜	亿	3'		清角	mi
F4	仉	生	4'		清变徵	fa
G4	伕	伏	5'		清徵	sol
A5	伍	仜	6'		清羽	la
B5	亿	伝	7'		清变宫	ti

TABLE 28 GŌNGCHĚ (工尺) AND JIǍNPǓ (简谱) NOTATION

In the Step Names (Jiēmíng, 阶名) there are additional notes: namely, a sharp fa (#4) called Zhōng (中), and a sharp la (#6) called Rùn (闰). Also, the five-tone system note for fa, Biànzhǐ (变徵), is called hé (和) in the step names.

In Step Names, (Jiēmíng, 阶名) the notes Gōng (宫), Shāng (商), Jiǎo (角), Zhǐ (徵), and Yǔ (羽) are authentic notes (Zhèngshēng, 正声). The notes Hé (和), Zhōng (中), Rùn (闰), and Biàn (变) are Changing Notes (Biànshēng, 变声).

TUNING SYSTEMS

While this notebook is based on using the scales in Western Twelve-Tone Equal Temperament system (12TET) this is a quick background of the Chinese tuning system.

The tuning systems are more complex and varied than shown here. I have only shown some of the main systems in use.

There are two tuning systems used. The first was originally called lǜlǚ (律呂) to represent the twelve bamboo pitch pipes. But more recently it is called Shí'èr lǜ (十二律) for 12 tones. This pitch system is used only to set the starting pitch of the root note of the scale.

The second system is used to define pitches of the actual music in the tune. The root note is Gōng (宮) and has the pitch defined by the first system. The remining notes now have their pitches defined by the Pythagorean tuning system.

This second system is called five tone or five modes. I use the term five tones in this notebook. It is a moving solfège style system and is technically equivalent to the European system.

PITCH STANDARDS

The setting of pitch is a complex issue not only because of the technical limitations of the physics and the maths involved but also because of competing personal, local and national interests.

It was not possible to measure pitch until the 1830's.

In the West, pitch standards have varied widely over time and from place to place. Competing standards arose, if only because people set the pitch locally and had no need or even the ability to conform to a standard. As music because more of a national and international endeavour, and as the technical capability increased, standards were proposed and a argued about. Two major standard pitches that came to be were setting the concert pitch to of A to 435 Hz. This was ratified first by the French and then agreed at the Conference of Vienna in 1885 to be used by some European nations. It was agreed again in the Treaty of Versailles (1919) to be used by the Germany and the Allies. But it never became an international standard.

In parallel the British Empire and USA a concert pitch of 440 Hz became the standard. This setting was eventually agreed to in 1955 in the ISO Standard ISO 16. Even to this day the pitch of A in Western Music varies from place to place. Generally, concert pitch is in the range 435 to 445 Hz.

In China, pitch standards were a similar issue. Each dynasty redefined the pitch standard and sometimes many pitch standards were used in different places or for different music. Unlike in the west where A is the standard across the board, the Chinese have 12 pitch standards, one standard for each of the 12 Tones. In part, this is because the Chinese never adopted the Twelve Tone-Equal-Temperament system. The Chinese pitch standard defines the pitch of the tonic note of the scale and is selected at the start of the piece of music.

In the western world, a tuning fork became the standard way of setting pitch, though orchestras still set their pitch to the oboe. In China the pitch was set by the tuning piper or by standard bells.

TUNING (SHÍÈRLÙ, 十二律)

Huáng Zhōng (黃鐘) is the equivalent of the Western C note. It is the starting point for the twelve-tone system. The Lǚ system is the oldest we know about. It is derived from adding and removing the third of the length of a pitch pipe to get the additional tones. The actual frequencies of the base note were generally set by a set of bells.

Note	SHÍÈRLÙ			Lǚ Ratio	Cents	12 TET
1	黃	黄钟	Huáng Zhōng	1:1	0.0	0
#1	大	大吕	Dà Lǚ	2187:2048	113.7	100
2	太	太簇	Tài Cù	9:8	203.9	200
#2	夾	夹钟	Jiá Zhōng	19683:16384	317.6	300
3	姑	姑洗	Gū Xiǎn	81:64	407.8	400
4	仲	仲吕	Zhòng Lǚ	177147:131072	521.5	500
#4	蕤	蕤賓	Ruí Bīn	729:512	611.7	600
5	林	林钟	Lín Zhōng	3:2	702.0	700
#5	夷	夷則	Yí Zé	6561:4096	815.6	800
6	南	南吕	Nán Lǚ	27:16	905.9	900
#6	无	无射	Wú Yì	59049:32768	1019.6	1,000
7	应	应钟	Yìng Zhōng	243:128	1109.8	1,100
+1	黃	黄钟	True Octave	2:1	1,200.0	1,200

TABLE 29 SHÍ'ÈRLÙ (十二律) TUNING

Modern Western musical instruments are tuned using Twelve-Tone Equal Temperament. Mathematically the notes in this tuning system are equally spaced according to the mathematical equation of the twelfth root of two ($\sqrt[12]{2}$) defining the space of a semitone. Historically the Chinese did know about using the $\sqrt[12]{2}$ to calculate the pitch of a note. They worked this out before it was reinvented in the west. But the Chinese never adapted this equal temperament system it into their standard music system. In this book all the work uses twelve-tone equal temperament as it fits Western musical instruments and software.

Note that the Chinese system here will not produce a true octave ratio of 2:1 because it is impossible to use ratios of 1:3 to generate a ratio of 2:1. I just ignore this and assume a proper 2:1 ratio. The actual ratio for this system's octave is 1224 cents.

PYTHAGOREAN TUNING

Once the fundamental pitch of the tonic note is determined, the actual pitch of the note is determined using Pythagorean Tuning.

Note	Note		Ratio	Cents	12 TET
1	宮	Gōng	1:1	0.00	0.00
#1	变商	*Biànshāng*	*256:243*	*90.53*	*100.00*
2	商	Shāng	9:8	203.20	200.00
#2	变角	*Biànjiǎo*	*32:27*	*294.93*	*300.00*
3	角	Jiǎo	81:64	405.70	400.00
4	变徵	Biànzhǐ[12]	4:3	498.49	500.00
#4	变征	Biànzhēng	1024:729	623.87	600.00
5	徵	Zhǐ	3:2	701.20	700.00
#5	变羽	*Biànyǔ*	*128:81*	*794.94*	*800.00*
6	羽	Yǔ	27:16	903.20	900.00
#6	闰	*Rùn*	*16:9*	*997.74*	*1,000.00*
7	变宫	Biàngōng	243:128	1,104.76	1,100.00
+1	上宮	Shànggōng	2:1	1,200.00	1,200.00

TABLE 30 PYTHAGOREAN TUNING

Note that while I have treated the enharmonic notes as being the same in this table, strictly speaking they are not the same.

Biàn (变) lowers the note down a quarter tone, semi tone, or tone.
Qīng (清) raises the note a quarter tone, semi tone, or tone. In some notations it also raises the note an octave, but I am avoiding this confusion in this book.
Shàng (上) is not officially used to raise the note an octave, but this is what I am using as it is a nice opposite to the use of xià (下) to lower the note an octave.
Zhuó (浊) or xià (下) lowers the note an octave.

The entries in this table in *italics* are ones I have added to complete the series. They are not officially part of the system.

---

[12] In some notations the 4th note is Hé (和) and the #4th note is Biànzhǐ (变徵).

GLOSSARY OF TERMS

Throughout this book I have used the modern simplified Chinese character set. In this table the terms are listed with both the traditional and simplified character sets.

鞍桥	Ānqiáo is the raised rear part of a horse's saddle. In music is refers to a Tone Group that starts and ends on the same note or an adjacent note.
八板	Bā Bǎn - Eight Beat – A Mother Tune or Bone Tune structure of 68 measures being 8+8+8+8+12+8+8+8 measures long.
八音之樂 / 八音之乐	Bā yīn zhī yuè - Eight Tone Music is the 12-tone system used in China. The eight tones refer to the materials the instruments were made from: metal 金, stone 石, clay 土, leather 革, silk 丝, wood 木, gourd 匏, and bamboo 竹. In this case Tone refers to the timbre or quality of the sound rather than the pitch of the sound.
百戏	Bǎixì is the meter of the music.
板	Bǎn - Fast or strong or short beat.
板式	Bǎnshì – Tempo or meter
八十四调 / 八十四調	Bāshísì diào - Eighty-Four Musical Modes
本套	Běntào is a simple 曲牌 qǔpái suite.
变 / 變	Biàn – to flatten a note. Usually a semi-tone.
变 / 變	Biàn lowers the note by a semitone or tone. In 阶名 jiēmíng (step names) biàn is a sharp 6 note.
變宮 / 变宫	Biàngōng is the seventh note in Five-Tone notation.
變宮樂 / 变宫乐	Biàngōngyuè is a Hexatonic Scale with the notes 1, 2, 3, 5, 6, 7.
變角 / 变角	Biànjiǎo is the sharp second note in Five-Tone notation. I have added this to fill in a gap in the notation.
變商 / 变商	Biànshāng is the sharp first note in Five-Tone notation. I have added this to fill in a gap in the notation.
变声 / 變聲	Biànshēng are Changing Notes in 阶名 Jiēmíng (step names). Changing Notes are notes that are not part of the pentatonic scale and should only be used as passing notes.
变套	Biàntào is another term used for the 变奏曲 Biànzòuqǔ variation form of the 曲牌 Qǔpái Suite.
變羽 / 变羽	Biànyǔ is the sharp five in Five-Tone notation. I have added this to fill in a gap in the notation.
變征 / 变征	Biànzhēng is a sharp 4th note in Five-Tone notation.
變徵 / 变徵	Biànzhǐ is note 4 in Five-Tone notation.
变奏曲 / 變奏曲	Biànzòuqǔ a suite with variations on a single theme.
变奏曲	Biànzòuqǔ is the variation form of the 曲牌 Qǔpái Suite.
毕曲	Bìqū is the last tune in a 曲牌 Qǔpái Suite.
Bone Tune	Bone Tune is a name for a tune that is an ostinato.
侧末眼	Cèmòyǎn – Final Beat Side making the third beat of a Tone Group longer. Expands one beat to one and a half or two beats.
侧头眼	Cètóuyǎn – Leading Beat Side making the first beat of a Tone Group longer. Expands one beat to one and a half or two beats.
抽眼	Chōuyǎn – Pinch Tune is a process of reducing the length of a standard tune by removing half the notes or removing whole phrases.

撮腔	Cuōqiāng is to sing two consecutive sixteenth notes in the first half of the last beat of the melisma.
大吕	Dà Lǚ – The second note in the Chinese Twelve-Tone system. Used here as C#3.
大锣	Dàluó is a large gong.
单排鼓	Dānpáigǔ is a single-skinned drum.
单皮鼓 / 單皮鼓	Dānpí gǔ is a single-skin drum (made of heavy circles of wood over which is stretched thick pigskin; the leading instrument in the orchestra in traditional opera, beating the time and thus having the other instruments play in unison).
打谱	Dǎpǔ is to modify the 曲牌 Qǔpái to fit the needs of a new lyric or melodic requirement.
垫腔	Diànqiāng is to add a leading note between a minor third and perfect fourth interval.
垫音	Diànyīn is a pad tone that fits between any tones separated by a minor third.
调	Diào means Mode as in the Chinese Mode System.
底板	Dǐbǎn is a percussive clapper that is used at the end of a melody to indicate that the melody has ended.
宫	Gōng is the first note of the Pentatonic Scale.
工尺谱/ 工尺谱	Gōngchě pǔ is a traditional Chinese music notation system.
宫调	Gōngdiào are the modes used in Chinese Music.
姑洗	Gū Xiǎn – The fifth note in the Chinese Twelve-Tone system. Used here as E3.
鼓点子	Gǔdiǎnzi is the beat of percussion instruments or a drumbeat.
和	Hé is a F in 阶名 Jiēmíng (step names) notation.
Heptatonic	Heptatonic is a scale that uses seven notes from the available twelve.
Hexatonic	Hexatonic is a scale that uses six notes from the available twelve.
黄鐘 / 黄钟	Huáng Zhōng – The first note in the Chinese Twelve-Tone system. Used here as C3.
夾鐘 / 夹钟	Jiá Zhōng – The fourth note in the Chinese Twelve-Tone system. Used here as D#/E♭3.
簡譜 / 简谱	Jiǎnpǔ is a Cypher Musical Notation System using the numbers 1 through 7 to describe the notes Do through Ti.
角	Jiǎo is the third note of the Pentatonic Scale.
截板	Jiébǎn is a clapper that strikes to indicate the end of a sung word or syllable.
阶名 / 階名 / 堦名]	Jiēmíng or step names is an old notation system.
紧拉慢唱	Jǐn lā màn chàng means fast playing with slow singing.
集曲	Jíqū is a 曲牌 Qǔpái that is modified by adding lines from a different 曲牌 Qǔpái.
九锤半 / 九錘半	Jiǔchuíbàn is the Nine and a Half Hammers Drum Pattern.
绝板	Juébǎn is a clapper that strikes to indicate the end of a sung word or syllable.
咔戏 / 咔戲 / 咔 戲	Kǎxì is a type of instrumental music that imitates an opera.
快板	KuaiBǎn – Fast Beat – allegro
龜茲	Kucha Scale (Qiūcí) is a scale used in eight tone music.
崑曲	Kūnqǔ – The oldest form of Chinese Opera.
扩板	Kuòbǎn doubles the length of the tune by adding extra 眼 yǎn beats every second beat.
联曲体 / 聯曲體	Liánqūtǐ in suites is the linked melody form.
联曲体	Liánqūtǐ is the linked melody form of the 曲牌 Qǔpái Suite.
林鐘 / 林钟	Lín Zhōng – The eighth note in the Chinese Twelve-Tone system. Used here as G3.

流水板	Liúshuǐbǎn is a fast and continuous rhythmic pattern.
乱锤 / 亂錘	Luànchuí is the disordered hammer drum pattern.
乱锤 / 亂錘	Luànchuí or disordered hammer is used to indicate a moment of confusion.
锣鼓经 / 鑼鼓經	Luógǔ jīng Drum is a type of drum and gong ensemble notation.
锣鼓点 / 鑼鼓點	Luógǔdiǎn – a fixed percussion pattern.
M2	Major second which is two semitones.
M7	Major seventh which is eleven semitones.
M6	Major sixth which is nine semitones.
M3	Major third which is four semitones.
慢板	mànbǎn – slow beat – lento
帽子头	Màozi tóu is a Drum Pattern.
马腿儿 / 馬腿兒	Mǎtuǐr is the Horse Leg Drum Pattern.
m2	Minor second which is one semitone.
m7	Minor seventh which is ten semitones.
m6	Minor sixth which is eight semitones.
m3	Minor third which is three semitones.
Mode	Mode is an overloaded term. In this book mode refers to the Chinese pentatonic modes. If the western modes are mentioned the term scale mode is used.
Mother Tune	Mother Tune is a name for a tune that is an ostinato.
南吕	Nán Lǚ – The tenth note in the Chinese twelve-tone system. Used here as A4.
铙钹	Náobó is a set of smallish Chinese crash cymbals.
拍	Pāi – beat or time
Pentatonic	Pentatonic is a scale that uses five notes from the available twelve.
P5	Perfect fifth which is seven semitones.
P4	Perfect fourth which is five semitones.
偏音级	Piān yīn jí are the two Changing Tones.
千声佛	QIĀN SHĒNG FÚ - A Thousand Buddhas. A Mother Tune with a structure of 15 beats.
腔头	Qiāngtóu is the note at the start of a melisma.
腔尾	Qiāngwěi is the note at the end of a melisma.
清	Qīng – to sharpen a note. Usually a semi-tone. It can also mean raising the note an octave.
清角	Qīngjiǎo is a Hexatonic Scale with the notes 1, 2, 3, 4, 5, 6
清乐 / 清樂	Qīngyuè is a Heptatonic Scale with the notes 1, 2, 3, 4, 5, 6, 7. This is the same as the Major Scale Ionian Mode.
全音五声音阶	Quányīn wǔ shēngyīn jiē is the Tonal Pentatonic Scale. (for Gong = C this would be C D E G A.)
曲调	Qǔdiào is a melody or a tune.
南蕤宾	Ruí Bīn Lǚ – The seventh note in the Chinese Twelve-Tone system. Used here as F#3.
闰	Rùn is a sharp sixth note (or flat seventh) in 阶名 Jiēmíng (step names) notation.
散板	Sǎnbǎn – Freely or irregular
散序	Sànxù is an unmetered prelude to a suite.
Scale Mode	Scale Mode is used to describe the modes of the western music system scales. This differentiates it from the term mode which refers to the Chinese modes.
闪板	Shǎnbǎn is a clapper that sounds before the start of melisma.
商	Shāng is the second note of the Pentatonic Scale.

十二律	SHÍ-ÈR-LÜ – The Chinese twelve-tone tuning system using ratios to approximate the twelfth root of two.
双键	Shuāngjiàn is typically used for double sword action. Two non-identical beats oscillate in a manner than shows harmony and coordination.
Spaced	Spaced chords are chords that follow a triad progression but there are no intervals of less than a triad.
太簇	Tài Cù – The third note in the Chinese twelve-tone system. Used here as D3.
Tone Singing	Tone singing is the use of a Melisma to provide information as to the tone of the word being sung.
同宫系统	Tóng gōng xìtǒng is the name of the system with 5 modes for each key.
TT	Tritone which is six semitones.
拖腔	Tuōqiāng is a melisma.
12 TET	Twelve Tone Equal Temperament.
無射 / 无射	Wú Yì – The eleventh note in the Chinese twelve-tone system. Used here as A4#.
下	Xià lowers the note an octave
险板	Xiǎnbǎn is a clapper that sounds before the start of melisma.
小锣	Xiǎoluó is a small gong.
旋宫	Xuán gōng rotating the tonic.
眼	Yǎn - Slow or weak or long beat.
眼	Yǎn – Slow or weak or long
燕乐 / 燕樂	Yànyuè is a heptatonic scale with the notes 1, 2, 3, 4, 5, 6, b7. This is the same as the major scale mixolydian mode.
摇板	Yáobǎn – Shaking or syncopated Beat
腰板	Yāobǎn is a clapper that sounds during a melisma.
雅乐 / 雅樂	Yǎyuè is a heptatonic scale with the notes 1, 2, 3, #4, 5, 6, 7. This is the same as the major scale lydian mode.
夷则	Yí Zé – The ninth note in the Chinese twelve-tone system. Used here as G#3.
一板七眼	yībǎn qīyǎn – one strong beat and seven weak beats. (notionally 8/4 time)
一板三眼	yībǎn sānyǎn – one strong beat and three weak beats. (notionally 4/4 time)
一板一眼	yībǎn yīyǎn - one strong beat and one weak beat. (notionally 2/4 time)
應鐘 / 应钟	Yìng Zhōng – The twelfth note in the Chinese twelve-tone system. Used here as B4.
應鐘 / 应钟	Yìng Zhōng the twelfth note in the Chinese twelve-tone system. Used here as B.
阴锣 / 陰鑼	Yīnluó is the Light Hurricane drum pattern.
引子	yǐnzi is the introduction to a 曲牌 qǔpái.
有板无眼	yǒubǎn wúbǎn – Strong beats only. (notionally 1/4 time)
羽	Yǔ is the fifth note of the pentatonic scale.
增板	Zēngbǎn is the resulting 8/4 metre than results from the doubling of a 4/4-meter phrase.
正版	Zhèngbǎn is a term indicating that the sung syllable occurs on the first beat of a phrase.
正声 / 正聲	Zhèngshēng are the authentic notes in 阶名 jiēmíng (step names) notation.
正音级	Zhèngyīn jí are the five positive pentatonic tones.
徵	Zhǐ is the fourth note of the pentatonic scale.
中	Zhōng is a sharp fourth note in 阶名 jiēmíng (step names) notation.
仲呂	Zhòng Lǚ – The sixth note in the Chinese twelve-tone system. Used here as F3.
中板	zhongbǎn – Medium beat – moderato
轉調	Zhuǎndiào is rotating of the mode.
浊 / 濁	Zhuó lowers the note an octave

子母调 / 子母調	Zǐmǔdiào is a term describing a type of alternating melody form.
子母調	Zǐmǔdiào is the alternating form of the 曲牌 qǔpái suite.
组曲 / 組曲	Zǔqǔ is a term describing the general suite form.

ABOUT MYSELF

I spent my early childhood in Singapore. In this time, I used to listen to my father and his friends sing Hakka Folk Songs. While I do not remember many songs, these folk songs and the Chinese pop songs of the times profoundly influenced my musical knowledge.

My family moved back to Australia and I was taught piano and trumpet in the standard Western Classical style. This book is my learnings about Chinese music theory but in the Western Musical System. I put it forth so others can also learn how to play Chinese music.

While my initial focus was Hakka Chinese folk music, this quickly had to expand into Chinese music in general. This notebook is primarily about the pentatonic scale, as used in Chinese music.

APPENDIX - 12 TET STEP TABLE

	C	C#	D	D#/Eb	E	F	F#	G	G#	A	A#	B	C
C	Unison												
C#	m2	Unison											
D	M2	m2	Unison										
D#/Eb	m3	M2	m2	Unison									
E	M3	m3	M2	m2	Unison								
F	P4	M3	m3	M2	m2	Unison							
F#	A4/d5	P4	M3	m3	M2	m2	Unison						
G	P5	A4/d5	P4	M3	m3	M2	m2	Unison					
G#	m6	P5	A4/d5	P4	M3	m3	M2	m2	Unison				
A	M6	m6	P5	A4/d5	P4	M3	m3	M2	m2	Unison			
A#	m7	M6	m6	P5	A4/d5	P4	M3	m3	M2	m2	Unison		
B	M7	m7	M6	m6	P5	A4/d5	P4	M3	m3	M2	m2	Unison	
C	P8	M7	m7	M6	m6	P5	A4/d5	P4	M3	m3	M2	m2	Unison
C#		P8	M7	m7	M6	m6	P5	A4/d5	P4	M3	m3	M2	m2
D			P8	M7	m7	M6	m6	P5	A4/d5	P4	M3	m3	M2
D#/Eb				P8	M7	m7	M6	m6	P5	A4/d5	P4	M3	m3
E					P8	M7	m7	M6	m6	P5	A4/d5	P4	M3
F						P8	M7	m7	M6	m6	P5	A4/d5	P4
F#							P8	M7	m7	M6	m6	P5	A4/d5
G								P8	M7	m7	M6	m6	P5
G#									P8	M7	m7	M6	m6
A										P8	M7	m7	M6
A#											P8	M7	m7
B												P8	M7
C													P8

APPENDIX - TEMPO TERMS

BPM	Western	Chinese	Romanised
	Prestississimo	极快的	jíkuàide
200 - 208	Prestissimo	最急板 （約為）	zuìjíbǎn (yuēwèi)
	Prestissimetto	風之速	fēngzhīsù
	Allegrissimo	快而活跃的	kuàiérhuóyuède
168 - 200	Presto	急板	jíbǎn
156-176	Vivace	活潑的	huópōde
	Allegro assai	颇快的	pǒkuàide
120 - 168	Allegro	快板	kuàibǎn
112–124	Allegro Moderato	适度, 中速的快板	shìdù, zhōngsùdekuàibǎn
104 - 112	Allegretto	小快板	xiǎokuàibǎn
90 - 115	Moderato	中板	zhongbǎn
80-108	Andantino	小行板 (比行板稍快)	xiǎoxíngbǎn (bǐxíngbǎnshāokuài)
76 - 108	Andante	行板	xíngbǎn
72 – 76	Adagietto	小柔板 / 頗慢	xiǎoróubǎn / pōmàn
66 - 76	Adagio	柔板	róubǎn
25-45	Grave	庄严的慢板	zhuāngyándemànbǎn
60 - 66	Larghetto	小慢板	xiǎomànbǎn
40 - 60	Lento	慢板	Mànbǎn
40 - 60	Largo	最缓板 / 或廣板	zuìhuǎnbǎn / huòguǎngbǎn
	Lentissimo	甚缓	shénhuǎn
<25	Larghissimo	极端地缓慢	Jíduāndehuǎnmàn

APPENDIX – CIRCLE OF FIFTHS

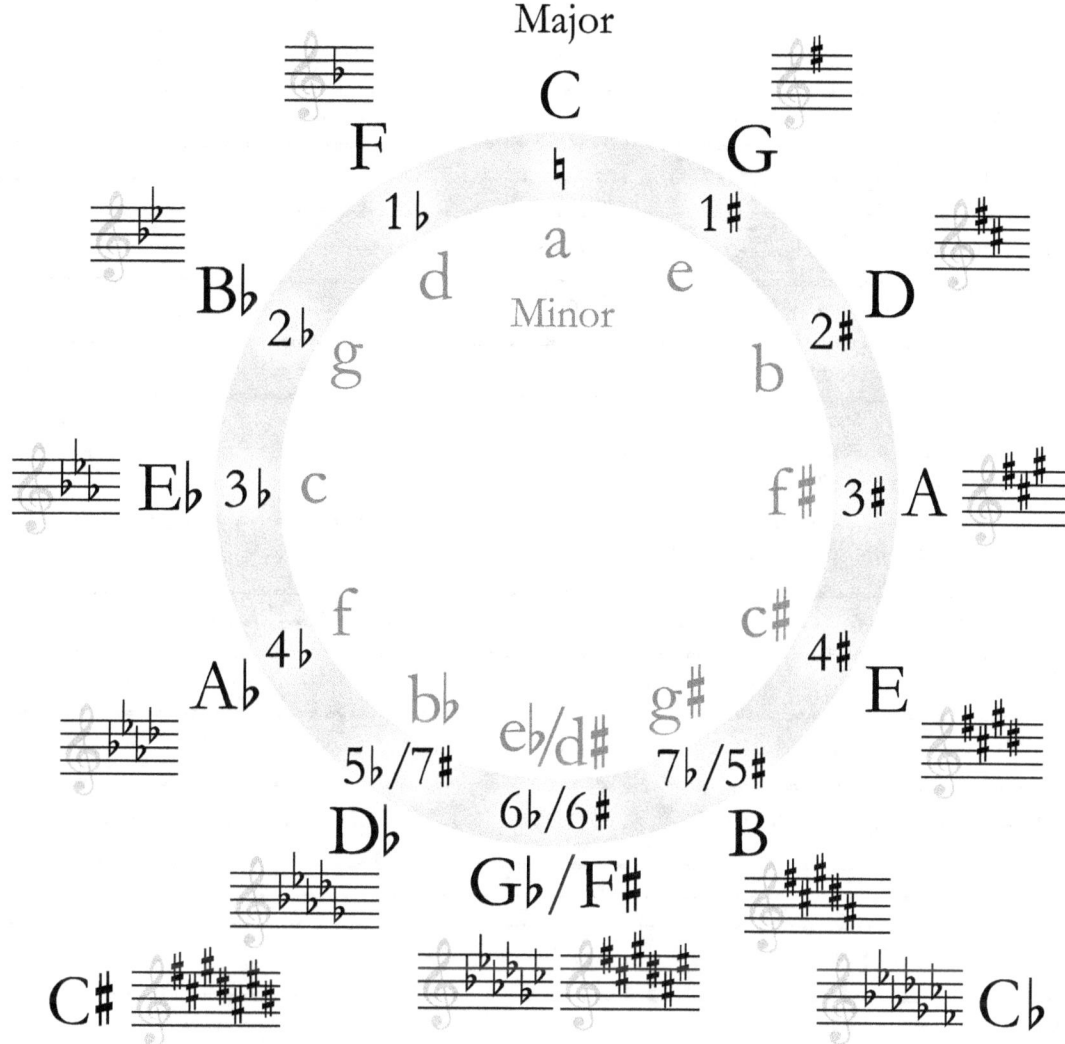

This circle of fifths diagram is from the Wikipedia user Just Plain Bill and is Licenced under the CC BY-SA 3.0 licence. No changes have been made.

TABLE OF CONTENTS

Introduction 1
What is Chinese Music? 1

Chinese Scales (Shēngyīn Jiē - 聲音階) 3

pentatonic scales (Wǔ Yīnjiē, 五音階) 3
Tonal Pentatonic Scale (Quányīn wǔ shēngyīn jiē, 全音五聲音階) 3
Other Pentatonic Scales 3
Heptatonic and Hexatonic Scales 6
hexatonic scales (Zhèngyīn jí, 正音级) 6
heptatonic scales (Tóng jūn sān gōng, 同均三宫) 7

Chinese note names 8
Music Key (Shí'èr lǜ, 十二律) 8
five tone note names (Zhèngyīn Jí, 正音级) 9

mode system (Tóng gōng xìtǒng, 同宫系统) 10

chords 11
C key Chords (Huáng Zhōng, 黄钟) - C Tonic – Gōng Mode (宫调) 11
Quartal Chords 12

Pentatonic Intervals 13
intervals – seconds 13
intervals – Thirds 13
intervals - Fifths 13
intervals – sixths 13

Pentatonic modes (Gōngdiào, 宫调) 14
C Key modes (Huáng Zhōng Lǜ, 黄钟律) 15
C Key intervals (Huáng Zhōng Lǜ, 黄钟律) 15
C Key chords (Huáng Zhōng Lǜ, 黄钟律) 16
C Key scales (Huáng Zhōng Lǜ, 黄钟律) 17

C# key modes (Dà Lǚ Lǜ, 大吕律)	18
C# key intervals (Dà Lǚ Lǜ, 大吕律)	18
C# key chords (Dà Lǚ Lǜ, 大吕律)	19
C# key scales (Dà Lǚ Lǜ, 大吕律)	20
d Key modes (Tài Cù Lǜ, 太簇律)	21
d Key intervals (Tài Cù Lǜ, 太簇律)	21
d Key chords (Tài Cù Lǜ, 太簇律)	22
d Key scales (Tài Cù Lǜ, 太簇律)	23
d# key modes (Jiá Zhōng Lǜ, 夹钟律)	24
d# key intervals (Jiá Zhōng Lǜ, 夹钟律)	24
d# key chords (Jiá Zhōng Lǜ, 夹钟律)	25
d# key scales (Jiá Zhōng Lǜ, 夹钟律)	26
e key modes (Gū Xiǎn Lǜ, 姑洗律)	27
e key intervals (Gū Xiǎn Lǜ, 姑洗律)	27
e key chords (Gū Xiǎn Lǜ, 姑洗律)	28
e key scales (Gū Xiǎn Lǜ, 姑洗律)	29
f key modes (Zhòng Lǚ Lǜ, 仲吕律)	30
f key intervals (Zhòng Lǚ Lǜ, 仲吕律)	30
f key chords (Zhòng Lǚ Lǜ, 仲吕律)	31
f key scales (Zhòng Lǚ Lǜ, 仲吕律)	32
f# Key modes (Ruí Bīn Lǜ, 蕤宾律)	33
f# Key inervals (Ruí Bīn Lǜ, 蕤宾律)	33
f# Key chords (Ruí Bīn Lǜ, 蕤宾律)	34
f# Key scales (Ruí Bīn Lǜ, 蕤宾律)	35
g key modes (Lín Zhōng Lǜ, 林钟律)	36
g key intervals (Lín Zhōng Lǜ, 林钟律)	36
g key chords (Lín Zhōng Lǜ, 林钟律)	37
g key scales (Lín Zhōng Lǜ, 林钟律)	38
g# key modes (Yí Zé Lǜ, 夷则律)	39

g# key intervals (Yí Zé Lǜ, 夷则律)	39
g# key chords (Yí Zé Lǜ, 夷则律)	40
g# key scales (Yí Zé Lǜ, 夷则律)	41
a Key modes (Nán Lǚ Lǜ, 南吕律)	42
a Key intervals (Nán Lǚ Lǜ, 南吕律)	42
a Key chords (Nán Lǚ Lǜ, 南吕律)	43
a Key scales (Nán Lǚ Lǜ, 南吕律)	44
a# key modes (Wú Yì Lǜ, 无射律)	45
a# key intervals (Wú Yì Lǜ, 无射律)	45
a# key chords (Wú Yì Lǜ, 无射律)	46
a# key scales (Wú Yì Lǜ, 无射律)	47
b key modes (Yìng Zhōng Lǜ, 应钟律)	48
b key intervals (Yìng Zhōng Lǜ, 应钟律)	48
b key chords (Yìng Zhōng Lǜ, 应钟律)	49
b key scales (Yìng Zhōng Lǜ, 应钟律)	50
progressions	**51**
2 note scale progressions	51
3 note scale progressions	51
4 note scale progressions	51
5 note scale progressions	51
Harmony	**52**
Switching keys	**53**
Beat and Time (Pāi, 拍)	**54**
Beat Groupings (节拍组, Jiépāi Zǔ)	**55**
Phrase Length 8 – Grouping 2+2+2+2	56
Phrase Length 8 – Grouping 2+2+4	56
Phrase Length 8 – Grouping 2+3+3	56
Phrase Length 8 – Grouping 2+4+2	56
Phrase Length 8 – Grouping 2+6	56
Phrase Length 8 – Grouping 3+2+3	56

Phrase Length 8 – Grouping 3+3+2	*57*
Phrase Length 8 – Grouping 3+5	*57*
Phrase Length 8 – Grouping 4+4	*57*
Phrase Length 8 – Grouping 5+3	*57*
Phrase Length 8 – Grouping 6+2	*57*
Phrase Length 12 – Grouping 2+2+2+2+2+2	*57*
PHRASE LENGTH 12 – GROUPING +2+2+2+3+3	*57*
PHRASE LENGTH 12 – GROUPING +2+2+3+2+3	*57*
PHRASE LENGTH 12 – GROUPING +2+3+2+2+3	*58*
PHRASE LENGTH 12 – GROUPING +3+2+2+2+3	*58*
PHRASE LENGTH 12 – GROUPING +3+2+2+3+2	*58*
PHRASE LENGTH 12 – GROUPING +3+2+3+2+2	*58*
PHRASE LENGTH 12 – GROUPING +3+3+2+2+2	*58*
PHRASE LENGTH 12 – GROUPING +2+2+2+2+4	*58*
PHRASE LENGTH 12 – GROUPING +2+2+2+4+2	*58*
PHRASE LENGTH 12 – GROUPING +2+2+4+2+2	*58*
PHRASE LENGTH 12 – GROUPING +2+4+2+2+2	*58*
PHRASE LENGTH 12 – GROUPING +4+2+2+2+2	*59*
PHRASE LENGTH 12 – GROUPING +2+2+4+4	*59*
PHRASE LENGTH 12 – GROUPING +2+4+2+4	*59*
PHRASE LENGTH 12 – GROUPING +4+2+2+4	*59*
PHRASE LENGTH 12 – GROUPING +4+2+4+2	*59*
PHRASE LENGTH 12 – GROUPING +4+4+2+2	*59*
PHRASE LENGTH 12 – GROUPING +2+3+3+4	*59*
PHRASE LENGTH 12 – GROUPING +2+3+4+3	*59*
PHRASE LENGTH 12 – GROUPING +2+4+3+3	*59*
PHRASE LENGTH 12 – GROUPING +4+2+3+3	*60*
PHRASE LENGTH 12 – GROUPING +4+3+2+3	*60*
PHRASE LENGTH 12 – GROUPING +4+3+3+2	*60*
PHRASE LENGTH 12 – GROUPING +3+2+3+4	*60*
PHRASE LENGTH 12 – GROUPING +3+2+4+3	*60*
PHRASE LENGTH 12 – GROUPING +3+4+2+3	*60*
PHRASE LENGTH 12 – GROUPING +4+3+2+3	*60*
PHRASE LENGTH 12 – GROUPING +4+2+3+3	*60*

PHRASE LENGTH 12 – GROUPING +4+3+3+2	60
PHRASE LENGTH 12 – GROUPING +3+3+2+4	61
PHRASE LENGTH 12 – GROUPING +3+3+4+2	61
PHRASE LENGTH 12 – GROUPING +2+3+4+3	61
PHRASE LENGTH 12 – GROUPING +3+4+3+2	61
PHRASE LENGTH 12 – GROUPING +4+4+4	61
PHRASE LENGTH 12 – GROUPING +8+2+2	61
PHRASE LENGTH 12 – GROUPING +2+8+2	61
PHRASE LENGTH 12 – GROUPING +2+2+8	61
PHRASE LENGTH 12 – GROUPING +8+4	61
PHRASE LENGTH 12 – GROUPING +4+8	62

Tone Groups ... 63

tone singing (Tuōqiāng, 拖腔) ... 64

tone group expansions ... 65

Rhythmic groups ... 67

Percussion (Luógǔdiǎn, 锣鼓点) ... 67

percussion as Background Ambience ... 68

    Riot of Hammers (luànchuí, 乱锤) ... 68

Nine and a half Hammers (jiǔchuíbàn, 九锤半) ... 68

    Light Hurricane (yīnluó, 阴锣) ... 69

    Skewer (chuànzi, 串子) ... 69

    Four Head strikes (Sìjītóu, 四击头) ... 70

    Horse Leg (Mǎtuǐ, 马腿) ... 70

Percussion as Punctuation ... 70

rhythmic Cues ... 71

Drum Notation (Luógǔ Jīng, 锣鼓经) ... 71

Melodies and Chords ... 73

    C Key chords (Huáng Zhōng, 黄钟) ... 75

    C# Key chords (Dà Lǚ, 大吕) ... 76

    D Key Chords (Tài Cù, 太簇) ... 77

    D# Key Chords (Jiá Zhōng, 夹钟) ... 78

E Key Chords (Gū Xiǎn, 姑洗)	79
F Key Chords (Zhòng Lǚ, 中吕)	80
F# Key chords (Ruí Bīn, 蕤宾)	81
G Key Chords (Lín Zhōng, 林钟)	82
G# Key Chords (Yí Zé, 夷则)	83
A Key Chords (Nán Lǚ, 南吕)	84
A# Key Chords (Wú Yì, 无射)	85
B Key Chords (Yìng Zhōng, 应钟)	86

short note instrument arpeggios ... 87

repeats (one note arpeggios)	87
trills (two note arpeggios)	87
Three note arpeggios	88
1-2-3 arpeggio	88
1-2-5 Arpeggio	89
1-2-6 Arpeggio	90
1-3-5 Arpeggio	91
1-3-6 Arpeggio	92
1-5-6 Arpeggio	92

Short Note Instrument Chords ... 93

Three Note Chords	93
Four Note Chords	94

Melodies (Qǔpái, 曲牌) and Suites (zǔqǔ, 组曲) ... 96

Suite Forms (zǔqǔ, 组曲)	96
Eight BEATS (Bābǎn, 八板)	97
A thousand buddhas (Qiān shēng fú, 千声佛)	98
Jasmine Flower Piano Arrangement (Mòlìhuā, 茉莉花)	99

Inverse scale modes ... 100

historical background ... 100

Notation Systems ... 100

Tuning Systems ... 102

Pitch Standards	102
Tuning (Shí'èrlǜ, 十二律)	103

pythagorean Tuning	*104*
Glossary of Terms	*105*
About Myself	*110*
Appendix - 12 TET Step table	*111*
Appendix - Tempo Terms	*112*
Appendix – circle of fifths	*113*

FIGURES

Figure 1 C key chromatic circle	16
Figure 2 C# Key Chromatic circle	19
Figure 3 D Key Chromatic Circle	22
Figure 4 D# key Chormatic Circle	25
Figure 5 E key Chormatic Circle	28
Figure 6 F key Chormatic Circle	31
Figure 7 F# key Chormatic Circle	34
Figure 8 G key Chormatic Circle	37
Figure 9 G# key Chormatic Circle	40
Figure 10 A key Chormatic Circle	43
Figure 11 A# key Chormatic Circle	46
Figure 12 B key Chormatic Circle	49

TABLES

Table 1 Steps for each Scale Mode	5
Table 2 Twelve Pipe Tuning Tonic Notes	8
Table 3 Five Tone Note Names	9
Table 4 Chinese Modes	10
Table 5 Mode Comparison	10
Table 6 Basic Chords	11
Table 7 C Key Chords	16
Table 8 C# Key Chords	19
Table 9 D Key Chords	22
Table 10 D# Key Chords	25
Table 11 E Key Chords	28
Table 12 F Key chords	31
Table 13 F# Key Chords	34
Table 14 G Key Chords	37
Table 15 G# Key Chords	40
Table 16 A Key Chords	43
Table 17 A# Key Chords	46
Table 18 B Key Chords	49
Table 19 Harmonic Notes	52
Table 20 Beat and Tempo	55
Table 21 Rhthmic Punctuation	70
Table 22 Single Instrument Percussion Notes	72
Table 23 Ensemble Percussion Notes	72
Table 24 Positive Pentatonic Chords	74
Table 25 Three Note Arpeggios	88
Table 26 Arpeggio Sequences	88
Table 27 Scale Inversions	100
Table 28 Gōngchě (工尺) and Jiǎnpǔ (简谱) Notation	101
Table 29 Shí'èrlǜ (十二律) TUNING	103
Table 30 Pythagorean Tuning	104

www.ingramcontent.com/pod-product-compliance
Lightning Source LLC
Chambersburg PA
CBHW050717090526
44588CB00014B/2320